TWAYNE'S WORLD AUTHORS SERIES

A Survey of the World's Literature

Sylvia E. Bowman, Indiana University

GENERAL EDITOR

FRANCE

Maxwell A. Smith, Guerry Professor of French, **Emeritus**
The University of Chattanooga
Visiting Professor in Modern Languages
The Florida State University

EDITOR

Rabelais

(TWAS 11)

TWAYNE'S WORLD AUTHORS SERIES (TWAS)

The purpose of TWAS is to survey the major writers —novelists, dramatists, historians, poets, philosophers, and critics—of the nations of the world. Among the national literatures covered are those of Australia, Canada, China, Eastern Europe, France, Germany, Greece, India, Italy, Japan, Latin America, New Zealand, Poland, Russia, Scandinavia, Spain, and the African nations, as well as Hebrew, Yiddish, and Latin Classical literatures. This survey is complemented by Twayne's United States Authors Series and English Authors Series

The intent of each volume in these series is to present a critical-analytical study of the works of the writer; to include biographical and historical material that may be necessary for understanding, appreciation, and critical appraisal of the writer; and to present all material in clear, concise English—but not to vitiate the scholarly content of the work by doing so.

Rabelais

By MARCEL TETEL

Duke University

Twayne Publishers, Inc. :: New York

To Joan

Preface

As in the case of any author who has a meaningful stature, it is most difficult to embrace all of Rabelais at any given time. When we think that we have dominated one of his facets, he slyly escapes our grasp. Fortunately, the search or chase continues, and one will never meet with complete success. Like a phoenix, Rabelais constantly renews himself for each succeeding generation.

In the following study, we do not, nor can we, pretend to have discovered the magic formula to Rabelais's works, or what he calls the "substantific marrow." Our thesis, however, is that his books, as any literary creation, have to be considered as an art form; unfortunately such an evaluation usually receives the least attention. Of course, Rabelais abounds in ideas, but the critic cannot merely consider them per se; he has to show how form reinforces content. Furthermore, certain ideas lose their timeliness, then the transcendental artistic values come to the foreground. In Rabelais such concepts as religious tolerance, education, utopias, just peace vs. senseless war, or marriage vs. cuckoldry cannot long remain the basis for a true literary masterpiece. Sometimes these notions are even abstracted into philosophical or religious systems by critics and, as a result, reach a dialectical deadend. If a specific work of literature survives the devastating erosion of time, esthetic instead of ideological criteria prevail when the fusion of the two disintegrates.

The *Fifth Book* of Rabelais is omitted because of the question of authenticity which surrounds it. At present, the general consensus of opinion is that the first sixteen chapters have the master's imprint, but that the remainder of the book belongs either to some imitator or appears in a very rough and plagiarized form which Rabelais did not have time to refine. Unless some document is found to substantiate the authenticity, the enigma may remain unresolved; any attempts to arrive at a conclusion from the interior of the work, that is through a stylistic or thematic comparison with the previous books, would amount to mere conjecture.

Quotations of Rabelais works are taken from Jacques Le Clercq's translation in the Modern Library Series. It does not represent the best edition available, but the most suitable for our purposes. The most acceptable translation, by Urquhart and Le Motteux, dates back to the seventeenth century; the fact that it would necessitate ample commentary and further translation indicates its quality and close relationship to the original. We have chosen the Le Clercq translation over several other modern ones because of its clear language; it also incorporates into the text any needed explanation or identification, thus eliminating distracting footnoting. On some occasions, when matters of style are discussed, we have taken the liberty of providing our own literal translation.

While various critical approaches and interpretations of Rabelais's books are given in the following study, this endeavor would have no true "raison d'être" if it did not attempt to present its own criteria to appreciate Rabelais. It does not claim to be evangelical, but discriminating in its approach to literature as a creation of intellect, imagination and beauty.

* * *

The following abbreviations are used after quotations:

| G | Gargantua | III | Third Book |
| P | Pantagruel | IV | Fourth Book |

The arabic numerals after these abbreviations refer to the chapter number.

Contents

Chronology

1494 Now the generally accepted date of François Rabelais's birth, although at times it has been pushed back as far as 1483. Born at La Devinière, a family property near Chinon, where his father, Antoine Rabelais, was a lawyer.

1511 Possible date for his entry into a monastery of the Franciscan order at Fontenay-le-Comte.

1525 Passes to the Benedictine Order with the hope that he can pursue more freely his humanistic studies.

1530 September 17—Rabelais registers at the school of medicine of the University of Montpellier.
November 1—receives his bachelor's degree in medicine.

1531 April 17 to June 24 gives lectures on Hippocrates and Galen. Toward the end of the year goes to Lyons.

1532 Publication of *Pantagruel* and the *Pantagrueline Prognostication*, a facetious almanac for the year 1533. Nominated doctor at the hospital of Hotel-Dieu (Lyons).

1533 *Pantagruel* is censured by the Sorbonne on October 23. November 8—Leaves for Italy with Cardinal Jean du Bellay as his personal secretary and doctor.

1534 February-March—Stay in Rome.
May—back in Lyons.
August—Publication of *Gargantua* (approximate date).

1535 Second trip to Rome with Jean du Bellay.

1536 July—Returns to Lyons and then departs for Paris with the Cardinal who is in charge of fortifying the capital against Charles V.

1537 Receives M.D. at Montpellier. Dissects the body of a hanged man.

1538 Death of Rabelais's son, Theodulus, at the age of two.

1540 Rabelais goes to Turin with Guillaume du Bellay, the Cardinal's eldest brother.

1542 December—returns to France with Guillaume du Bellay who will die before reaching his destination.

1543 The Sorbonne censures again *Gargantua* and *Pantagruel*.

1545 François I licenses Rabelais to publish another work.

1546 Publication of the *Third Book*. In spite of the license, a new censure forces Rabelais to seek refuge in Metz where he practices medicine.

1547 Rabelais comes back to Paris.
July—Leaves for Rome with Jean du Bellay. Passing through Lyons, he gives to the publisher the first eleven chapters of the *Fourth Book*.

1549 September—Rabelais sends back to the French court, specifically to the Duke de Guise, an account of the *Sciomachie*, a description of the festivities in Rome to celebrate the birth of an heir to Henri II.

1550 Rabelais receives an official license for the *Fourth Book*.

1551 Through the auspices of Cardinal du Bellay, Rabelais obtains the vicarship of two parishes, in other words, financial security.

1552 Publication of the *Fourth Book*.
March—Renewed harassment by the Sorbonne.

1553 Rabelais resigns from his two vicarships.
April (?)—Death of Rabelais.

1562 Publication of *L'Isle Sonante* (*Ringing Island*) usually considered of Rabelais's own hand.

1564 Publication of the *Fifth Book* whose first sixteen chapters compose the episode of Ringing Island.

CHAPTER 1

An Attempt at the Grotesque

IN 1532, the same year that marked the appearance of *Panta-gruel*, Rabelais published two scholarly texts and edited one esoteric document. Since he had become a doctor himself in 1530 and had then taught medicine at the leading French medieval university of Montpellier, it is not surprising that his first works were editions of Hippocrates' *Aphorisms* and Galen's *Medical Art* (*Ars medicinalis*). Later in 1532 he edited a will and contract dating back to antiquity which was later declared a hoax, much to his embarrassment: *Ex reliquiis venerandae antiquitatis. Lucii Cuspidii testamentum. Item contractus venditionis antiquis Romanorum temporibus initus.*

By its very nature *Pantagruel* clashes with the spirit of these learned works and shows a different facet of Rabelais, a facet through which he is now remembered (whereas the active scholar tends to be forgotten). Such a change in literary activity remains a leading enigma. Did Rabelais start writing popular literature because he knew it would sell well and thereby ease his financial difficulties? No known facts could substantiate such a hypothesis. Or did he finally give in to his natural inclinations, verve, and exuberance in order to find an endless outlet in this form of explosive literature while exposing the foibles of his time and perhaps venting some of his own feelings on matters which preoccupied his contemporaries? This last conjecture offers a more plausible explanation for his sudden about-face.

I *The Popular and Epic Traditions*

Rabelais derived the title of his first book from a relatively un-known source. The earliest mention of the name Pantagruel ap-pears in a fifteenth-century religious drama and the name reoccurs in several later plays. In these works Pantagruel represents a little devil who causes thirst in anybody whom he confronts; he will keep the same characteristic in Rabelais's book.[1] One wonders about the choice of such a figure for the main character of a book, although the popularity of medieval theater was still quite strong at the beginning of the sixteenth century. The title itself gives the best clue: *The Horrendous and Frightful Prowesses of the Renouned Pantagruel, King of the Dipsodes, Son of the big Giant Gargantua.* This last phrase clearly identified Pantagruel in the eyes of Rabelais's readers because they all knew very well the giant's father, Gargantua, as we shall see in the next chapter. Having read about Gargantua's many adventures, they now would eagerly follow the son's peregrinations.

Essentially *Pantagruel* adheres to the main lines of an epic or a romance of chivalry, continuing an already well-established literary tradition; the book is divided into three parts: the birth and the youth of the hero, his education, and his exploits. The *Song of Roland* inherited much from the *Iliad* and the *Aeneid* and in turn gave birth to a whole complex of literature which slowly degenerated as it crossed the Alps into Italy. Rabelais was influenced by such works from that country as *Il Morgante* by Luigi Pulci and *Baldus* by Teofilo Folengo, both of which were narratives about the prowess of giants and knights set in a Carolingian background.

Like Hector and Aeneas, Pantagruel, and later Gargantua, surrounds himself with a group of inseparable companions. Rabelais narrates long and involved battles, fuses the marvelous with the real, and takes the reader through a series of fantastic voyages and on a visit to Hell as Virgil had done before him. The epic praises the virtues of a nation and shows man trying to rival God. Had not Homer sung the praises of Greece, and did not Virgil immortalize the ambitions and the superiority of the Romans? Rabelais adheres only in a skeletal way to the epic or romance of chivalry structures; he has one long serious moment in the letter from Gargantua to Pantagruel in which the father suggests to his son how to take advantage of the vast source of knowledge which the Renaissance has rediscovered or re-evaluated. Otherwise the author either profits from the epic frame or creates a variety of episodes to give vent to his affinity for vulgarity and exaggeration. Through this vulgarity and exaggeration and through the epic framework, Rabelais sought to parody the epic and its later literary descendants. Since the epic and chivalrous literature of antiquity and the Middle Ages is held in awe and respect and is surrounded by a halo of poetry, downgrading it will produce parody.

To give its giant an aura of importance and respectability, *Pantagruel* begins with a genealogy of the main character. Some have held that Rabelais here wants to parody the genealogy of Christ found in the Bible, but such a device can also be noted in many accounts of heroes in ancient and medieval literature; therefore, one suspects that the author intended to imitate the latter literary tradition rather than to blaspheme Saint Matthew's Gospel.[2] The apostle himself must have adhered to a tradition begun by Homer. The almost interminable list of giants is derived from figures in mythology, the Bible, and medieval and early Renaissance literature (Morgan from Pulci's tale and Fracassus from Folengo's *Baldus*). Rabelais cannot satisfy his whim with a logical enumeration of giants; he has to string out the names to such an unwarranted degree that only cacophony emerges, and the unnecessary overaccumulation enhances the resulting grotesque. The heaping of names has made impossible any semblance of verisimilitude and has produced this grotesque: "Cacus begat Enceladus, who begat Ceus, who begat Typhoeus, who begat Aloeus, who begat Othus, who begat Aegeon. Aegeon begat Briareus, who had a hundred hands; who begat Porphyrio, who begat Adamstor, who begat Auteus, who begat Agatho, who begat Porus . . ." (*P*, 1).[3]

To conform to literary and popular tradition, Pantagruel was born at the time of the worst drought the world has ever witnessed. He saw the light after a rain that was saltier than brine; in the medieval play the little devil Pantagruel covered the sea with salt. Rabelais affects an air of scholarship and, using a burlesque etymology, gives the origin of the giant's name; this technique of the pseudo etymology has great appeal for the common reader and helps give the book a popular tone: "His father called him Pantagruel or All-Athirst, a name derived from the Greek 'Panta' meaning all, and the Hagarene or Saracen 'gruel' meaning athirst" (*P*, 3). The birth of mythological heroes was usually accompanied by extraordinary events which were good omens for their futures, but Rabelais transposes this tradition to a somewhat base level to underscore the burlesque and grotesque intent of the scene in vulgar and simplistic terms: "For while his mother Badebec was bringing him forth and the midwives stood by ready to receive him, there first issued from her belly seventy-eight salt-vendors, each leading a salt laden mule by the halter. They were followed by nine dromedaries, bearing hams and smoked oxtongues; seven camels bearing chitterlings; twenty-five cartloads of leeks, garlic, onions and chives. This terrified some midwives but others said: 'God help us, he is born hair and all. . . . He will do terrible wonders. If he lives, he will grow to a lusty age" (*P, 2*).

Exaggeration on a simple and evident level continues in the description of Pantagruel's youth and travels. Four thousand six hundred cows are needed to furnish milk to feed the infant giant. The chains which barred the entrance to the port of La Rochelle are used to tie the boisterous child to his crib; these chains were chosen because they inject an element of pseudoverisimilitude into the tale and make the account, therefore, all the more fantastic, but on a superficial plane. As he starts the traditional tour of universities, a medieval remnant, the same technique of geographical allusion is used; in Poitiers, Pantagruel builds the Pierre Levée, the Lifted Stone; a huge rock which the students climbed; then, after visiting Toulouse, Montpellier, Bourges and Orléans, he is credited with the construction of the Roman aqueduct called the Pont du Gard and the amphitheater of Nimes. Rabelais here pays homage to the universities and cities he himself probably attended or visited and at the same time caters to the taste of the majority of his readers; they expected and enjoyed Pantagruel's feats because they were familiar with the places described and were used to this technique from similar tales in great popularity at the time, but above all they took pleasure in having the author play with their credulity. Neither was fooling the other, though the author tried to catch the reader who adroitly escaped the trap.

In epic or chivalrous literature, it is the hero's duty to seek out or engage in combat in order to demonstrate his courage and virtue. In chivalrous literature, the knight will roam the country, fighting men, monsters, or giants to prove to his fair lady that he is worthy of her love. The epic hero will rise to the occasion to defend his native land against its enemies, or he will leave for far-flung exotic places to protect other lands and peoples from the forces of evil and injustice. Pantagruel, following the latter tradition, interrupts his education and starts out for Utopia (Sir Thomas More's work had appeared shortly before 1518) to protect it from its invaders, the Dipsodes (meaning the thirsty ones), and their giant mercenaries.

In the description of Pantagruel's defeat of the Dipsodes and the giants, Rabelais fuses the popular and the epic traditions, thereby appealing to a wider reading public. In an episode reminiscent of the role of the little devil in the medieval plays, Pantagruel sends to the Dipsodes a special "jelly" he has prepared which when eaten brings about an unquenchable thirst; later he will throw eight kegs of wine and four bushels of salt into the mouth of the giants' leader. Forced to drink so much wine, the giants will become easy prey. To add a touch of vulgarity and emphasize the element of Parody, Pantagruel drowns the Dipsodes with the deluge of his urinal flow.

Amidst this crude scene, Rabelais invokes the muses to inspire him before he proceeds to describe the defeat of the giants. By the use of this technique, so dear to the poets of antiquity, Rabelais pretends that he needs inspiration, but he only goes through the motions. When this invocation, set in a vulgar episode, is compared with the practice venerated in antiquity, parody results: "Oh, who on earth were able fitly to relate how Pantagruel demeaned himself against the threescore giants? O my muse, O Calliope, mother of epic song, and thou Thalia, with thy comic lyre, inspire me in this hour, restore my powers to me, for here is the 'pons asinorum' [difficulty] of logic; here is the stumbling block: how shall I sing the horrible battle that ensued" (*P*, 28).

The intercession of God at the beginning of the struggle between Pantagruel and Werewolf, the leader of the giants, is a direct imitation of epic literature: "Then there was heard a voice from Heaven saying: 'Hoc fac et vinces: do this and thou shalt conquer'" (*P*, 27). In Homer and Virgil, the gods constantly come to the rescue of the heroes. And did not God lengthen the day in an attempt to allow Charlemagne to rescue Roland? With this device Rabelais slyly elevates his tale to an epic level, but the combat that follows draws it back down to a popular and base plane. Pantagruel may have God on his side, but Werewolf's mace is enchanted by an evil fairy and therefore is indestructible. To further bring it within the reader's reach of mind and to plunge him into the grotesque, the mace weighs: "one million eighty six thousand six hundred and twenty four pounds, with at its end, thirteen pointed diamonds, the smallest of which was as great as the large bell of Notre Dame in Paris" (P, 29). Rabelais here makes use of a technique drawn from popular tradition that he will repeat many times; he playfully gives a very precise mathematical description of a gigantic number, as if it mattered.[4] Then in keeping with similar scenes in medieval and early Renaissance tales, Pantagruel, after defeating Werewolf, picks him up and whirls him as he would a pike to destroy the other giants.

If Rabelais does not succeed, but wilfully so, in elevating the scene to an epic level, he creates some happy artistic moments by means of similes which purposely denigrate the episode and paradoxically enhance the parody. At the same time these similes give the scene an independent life and momentarily take it out of its grotesque and crude context. They produce a sort of interplay between each of the giants and the objects to which he is compared, derogatory in the case of Werewolf and positive in the case of Pantagruel: "But Pantagruel dealt Werewolf such a vicious kick in the belly, that he fell backward, his heels over his head; then he proceeded to drag him tailscraping the length of a bowshot . . . Pantagruel picked up Werewolf by the feet and wielded his boy like a pike. . . . As for Pantagruel he looked like a mower who with his scythe (Werewolf himself) cut down the meadow grass (My Lords the giants). Pantagruel flung Werewolf hard as he could into the city. The giant landed on his belly (like a frog) in the middle of the main square" (P, 29).

No parody of the epic is complete without the inclusion of a visit to Hell. Did not Aeneas go to see his father Anchisus in Hades? Ingeniously Rabelais creates his own brand of this episode which no longer has anything in common with its ancestors; basically it will serve as an outlet for his imagination from which flows, in this case, a topsy-turvy universe. Epistemon, one of Pantagruel's companions, has been decapitated during the Werewolf struggle by a flying stone.[5] When he is resuscitated, his head is sealed back to his body with some "mysterious salve." Epistemon narrates that he saw in Hell the leaders of the world, and the heroes of mythology and literature, as well as some writers, engaged in the most abject and base occupations; only philosophers, who had always struggled through life, led a luxurious existence in the underworld: "Pyrrhus put terror into Roman ears with his huge elephants and won the day at Asculum; but little it profits him today as he washes dirty stew-pans. . . . Romulus ekes out a living as a saltmaker by repairing falderals. . . . John of Paris, hero of chivalry, is a greaser of boots; conversely King Arthur of Britain is an ungreaser of round hats . . . Pope Julius makes his way by crying meat pies. . . ." (*P*, 30). In addition to its satirical effect, the lengthy description of persons and their dismal occupations affords Rabelais an opportunity to let his verve flow freely. The parody or imitative effect of the episode is soon forgotten; what comes to the fore is a vast fresco swarming with grotesque figures. Rabelais has shown here his originality by a rather elementary process: contrasting the sublime and the vulgar; these historical figures, who commanded awe and respect, are downgraded to doing the most base and unusual jobs.

II Satirical Verbal Distortion

The line of demarcation between parody and satire often is not easily discerned. Parody imitates and denigrates, but it also mocks and criticizes; satire principally criticizes and mocks, and in doing so it too imitates and denigrates. The difference between the two is that the satirist aims to create a cathartic effect in the reader, but if the satire becomes too grotesque, his moralizing intent almost disappears. In *Pantagruel*, when Rabelais attacks the existing education system, exaggeration sets in immediately and soon satire retreats into the background.

During his peregrinations, Pantagruel meets a Limousin student in Orléans who greets him speaking a gallicized Latin in order to show off how much he has learned at the university. Most students of the time vitiated their speech with Latin affectations, and Rabelais certainly intends to criticize this practice. However, the episode becomes an opportunity for Rabelais to give way to his affinity for exaggeration, and he lets the student speak endlessly in this affected language.[6] A few sentences would suffice to make the point, but Rabelais constantly expands beyond the boundaries of the necessary; this verbal expansion distorts and purposely detracts from the original satirical meaning: "We transfretate the

Sequana [Seine] at the dilucul and crepuscul; we deambulate by the compites and quadrives of the metropolis; we despume the Latin verbocination and, like verisimilary amorabonds, we captate the benevolence of the omnijugal, omniform and omnigeneous muliebrine sex" (*P*, 6).

Rabelais continues to fire his volleys at scholasticism and education when he has Pantagruel enumerate for us the books found at the library of Saint Victor.[7] In this strictly imaginary list of books, the author uses some of his favorite techniques; he distorts titles by means of macaronic Latin, obscenity, and vulgarity; he puns continuously with words or images; he attributes real books to imagined authors and imagined books to real authors. All in all, these titles become puppets which jump and gesticulate before our eyes as Rabelais smiles behind the scene, proud of his accomplishment, now laughing at the weakness of his contemporaries, now laughing with us. The enumeration is a veritable *tour de force* not only because of the sheer accumulation of books but because each title represents a small universe full of suggestions and implications which we delight in deciphering: "*The Windbags of Rome*, Bricot: *De differentiis soupparum* (*Of the Difference in Soups* by Father Bricot, a priest of Notre Dame), *Humility, an Old Shoe*, *Reverendi patris fratris Lubini provincialis Bavardiæ, de croquendis Lardinobus libri tres* (*On guzzling Bacon*, in three volumes, by the Reverend Father Brother Gutcrammer, a Bavarian citizen) . . . *The Spectacles of Roman Pilgrims* . . . *The Prelates' Bagpipe* [allusion to their proverbial corpulence], *The Complaint of the Lawyers on the Reformation of Gratuities* . . ." (*P*, 7).

The basis of scholastic education resides in the debate. Soon after his arrival in Paris, Pantagruel is given the test to arbitrate a debate between Kissarse and Bumfondle. The names of the protagonists indicate from the outset what style the argumentation will take. Never will we know the exact topic of the pleadings, and it does not matter; what Rabelais has proposed to show is the absurdity which dominates the interminable argumentations by lawyers or theologians who take pleasure in hearing themselves and really do not care about the substance of their speeches. The result is a magnificently incoherent cock-and-bull verbiage; Kissarse drowns himself in a base jumble, and Bumfondle submerges in his own supercilious rhetoric.[8] Rabelais has again engaged in his favorite game of superfluous verbal play and exaggeration; he has re-created in his own image a supposedly satirical scene which is no longer anchored by a critical emphasis. As a matter of fact, he has sprung two marionettes who acquire vivid caricatural traits from their deformed exposition:

I laid the matter before the clerks, begging these gentlemen to examine it. They concluded *frisemorum*, according to the modes in the first figure of the syllogism, that nothing can compare with mowing in summer in a cellar provided with pen and ink, with paper and penknives from Lyons on the Rhone, tittuppy-tattuppy. It surely must be obvious that, the moment armor smells of garlic, rust eats it to the very liver? Besides, they do nothing but wrangle and brangle among themselves, inciting the wrynecks and headtwisters as they skim over the postprandial nap. That I insist, is what makes salt so dear (*P*, 12).

To give the scene a semblance of reality within an absurd context, Pantagruel judges the argument, and the two pleaders accept his judgment. Verisimilitude plays with the absurd and tries to overcome it, almost succeeding for a moment until we realize the overwhelming nature of the episode.

Rabelais graduates his satire by carrying *ad absurdum* the mania of argumentation. Words no longer suffice; the final debate between Panurge and Thaumastes, an English scholar (Sir Thomas More?), will take place by means of signs. Rabelais has plunged debating, the subject of his criticism, into the realm of the totally irrelevant in order to take a final blow at it. While he purposely reduces his view of his contemporaries to a neanderthalic level, he produces an episode which acquires an intrinsic value because of its grotesque, if not obscene, qualities. There is a logic in the detailed gesticulations of the "orators" when the movements are considered individually, but when they are pieced together no over-all meaning or continuity emerges from them. Only the delight of being led through an inextricable maze remains: "The Englishman raised an open left hand, made a fist, placed his thumb on the point of his nose. Then he quickly raised his right hand, open too, to bring it down and link his left little finger with his right thumb, moving the other fingers slowly through the air. He then repeated the operation, the right hand doing what the left hand had done, and conversely" (*P*, 19).

III *Gallic Salt and Freedom*

The sparkling light of *Pantagruel* is introduced in Panurge, a genial character whose various escapades occupy the bulk of the book. Panurge derives his name from the Greek *panourgos* ("all-powerful, who can do anything"), and he endeavors to live up to its meaning. Throughout Rabelais's work we shall see an apparent evolution of this character, but in *Pantagruel* he appears as an amoral much more than an immoral person, an individual who lives outside of society according to his own set of standards. He suffers from a perpetual sickness called "lack of money," and he stops at nothing to cure it:

Yet when he needed money, he knew thirty-three methods of acquiring it, the most ordinary and honorable of which was filching. . . . He was constantly plotting against the sergeants and the watch. . . . In his coat he had more than twenty-six pockets and pouches which were always full. One held a pair of loaded dice and a small knife like a glover's awl to cut purses with. . . . Another pocket held a lot of little packages filled with fleas and lice which he recruited from the tramps at the Saint Innocent's graveyard and cast with small sticks or quills down the backs of the smartest gentlewomen he could find (*P*, 16).

Although Panurge is Rabelais's original creation, he belongs to a certain literary tradition; he continues, and foreshadows as well, a lineage of this sort of character. He takes his place in the cunning and sly family of individuals who populate the *fabliaux* and the *Roman de Renart* of the Middle Ages. He has direct ancestors in Margutte, a leading figure in Pulci's *Morgante* and in Cingar (from the Italian *zingaro*, "*gypsy*"), the companion of Folengo's *Baldus*.[9] Panurge becomes the forerunner of Till Eulenspiegel, Molière's Scapin, Diderot's Rameau's Nephew, and Beaumarchais's Figaro.

When Pantagruel first meets Panurge in Paris, a magnetic and inseparable relationship is immediately formed between them. The giant asks him the basic questions that man has always asked himself and that Panurge will really try to answer, but not until the *Third Book:* "Who are you? Where are you going? What do you wish?" (*P*, 9). The meeting between the two is reminiscent of Pantagruel's encounter with the Limousin student. In pretending to answer the questions, Panurge unleashes against the giant an avalanche of languages: Latin, Greek, Germanic, Romance, and strictly imaginary (Utopian) tongues.[10] Panurge has succeeded in living up to his name and in showing off his knowledge, but above all, Rabelais has had an opportunity to overindulge himself in a huge accumulation of various jargons, based on real languages, which take on a sonorous playful value rather than a meaningful one:

Agonou dont oussoys vous denaguez algarou, nou den farou zamist vous mariston ulbrou, fousquez vous brol, tam bredaguez moupreton den goul houst, daguez daguez nou croupys fost barbounnoflist nou grou. Agou paston tol nalprissys bourtou los echatonous prou dhouquys brol panygou den bascrou noudous caguons goulfren goul oust troppassou. "I believe I understand him," said Pantagruel. "Either that language is my native Utopian or it is very much like it in sound" (*P, 9*).

From the very start, Panurge is depicted as a master of hoaxes, even in his encounter with Pantagruel, and basically he appears in this light throughout the book. For the most part, his adventures consist of a series of tricks which he plays on various individuals, including his "debate" with Thaumastes. He places stink bombs under the benches of the theologians from the Sorbonne; he mercilessly whips any page he meets on the street; he sews a priest's alb to his shirt, and when the latter wants to take off his ceremonial vestments, he finds himself undressed. Much of the Gallic salt for which Rabelais is renowned can be found in Panurge's actions or speeches, not only in *Pantagruel*, but in the other books as well.[11] Because of the predominance of hoaxes and trickery, *Pantagruel* follows very closely the medieval tradition of the *fabliau*. Although elementary, these techniques are effective in obtaining comic situations. Someone falls in a trap, and we laugh because we find ourselves superior to the victim; we know of the victim's forthcoming plight, but he does not. However, we must remain objective and not sympathize with him or all comic effects disappear. Much of medieval popular literature was based on this sort of lighthearted cruelty.

The question that has attracted the most attention concerning Panurge's character is whether he is a courageous or a cowardly individual. In *Pantagruel*, he shows a blatant arrogance and audacity, although on one or two occasions he does display some natural cowardice (when he is chased by the police, and when a woman whom he wants to assail cries out for help); in other words, if his behavior reminds one of students' pranks, it also follows a normal pattern of reactions. The most grotesque episode in relation to Panurge occurs in the description of his escape from the Turks; like some of his literary ancestors, he claims a dubious, if not illegitimate, past in the Middle East: "Well, my Lord, those lewd Turks larded me like a rabbit (I was so thin my flesh would otherwise have provided a poor grade of meat), ran a spit through me and were grilling me alive. As I roasted, I recommended myself to the Divine Grace. Remembering good Saint Lawrence, I kept hoping that God would deliver me from this torment. As a matter of fact, that is exactly what happened—and in a very strange manner! to be sure!" (P, 14). His prayers finally answered, he escapes from his roaster by starting a fire; the scent of burning bacon on his body attracts dogs that he repels by picking pieces of roasted bacon off himself and throwing them at the animals. The episode is filled with an undertone of blasphemy if one chooses to see it as a parody of miracles or saints' lives, for example—but a stronger undercurrent of grotesque, although somewhat crude, sweeps away the apparent ripple of heresy. Above all, the significance of this chapter lies in the fact that it announces the imaginative and lively Rabelais, the storyteller of later books. He handles the narration with a verve unequaled anywhere else in *Pantagruel*.

Panurge remains a highlight of Rabelais's works because, unlike the other characters, he is an individual instead of a type, and he becomes more and more so. We envy him because he acts and speaks freely. He embodies our desires and weaknesses. If he were cast into modern society, he would come forth as a twentieth-century Meursault, Camus's protagonist in the *Stranger*, an outcast of society who exists in an absurd universe. One can safely assume that Rabelais created an amoral Panurge whose God takes the shape of a gratuitous act in order to free himself from his own frustrations and griefs: his fights with the Sorbonne, his loss of a child, and his revolt against his monastic background.[12] Rabelais projected himself in his idealized Panurge— an idealization by definition unattainable.

IV Sophomoric Giganticism

In ending *Pantagruel,* Rabelais reverts to the popular tradition, thereby completing a structural cycle, since the beginning of the book adhered mostly to the same tradition. This light and superficial ending might alleviate the slightly more complex episode of Werewolf, but Rabelais simply gives in to the exigencies of the trade; the readers expected more references to giganticism, and he had to satisfy these demands to make his work more salable. The book bears the name of the giant, but it is not until the end that Rabelais returns to this theme and, so to speak, pays lip service to it while practicing what will become a greater part of *Gargantua.* As a result, he creates a whole anthropomorphic universe; the giant contains a whole living world into which the author himself, under the pseudonym and anagram of Alcofribas Nasier, travels and discovers a wondrous land: "Leaving hastily, I passed along the rock of his teeth and kept walking until I got to the top of one. Here I found the fairest pleasure resort in the world, with large tennis courts, spacious galleries, sweet meadows, plentiful vines and an infinity of pretty houses, built Italian-fashion in the midst of delightful verdure. Here I spent a good four months and never fared better in my life" (*P,* 32).

Later when Pantagruel becomes ill, huge laxative pills are lowered into his stomach; each pill contains several men whose care—they proceed immediately to scour and flush his digestive tract—soon cures him. The device of toying with giganticism produces pleasant but simplistic effects; in keeping with the tone of the book, the gigantic abyss remains on a playful level and does not become a frightening or mysterious world.[13] The grotesque, issuing from such an exaggerated representation, has no real sophistication; it emanates from a rather puerile and unimaginative concept of giganticism.

Many have reproached Rabelais for terminating *Pantagruel,* and some of his other books, in an abrupt manner. It is true that he suddenly declares: "I will leave off here because my head aches a little and I realize that the registers of my brain are somewhat blurred by this septembral mash. (As you well know, new wine is heady)" (*P,* 34). He is accused of skimping on the job; having run out of material or imagination, he has to finish the book one way or another. Certainly in later years while making other revisions, Rabelais could have modified the ending if he had chosen to do so. Consequently, there must be a purpose in this so-called fizzled ending, especially since the other books also terminate in a more or less illogical fashion. Rabelais chooses to end *Pantagruel* abruptly with a confusing jumble that is in keeping with the popular tone of the work. He wants to leave us with a last impression of irreality and irrelevance; in other words, he continues to play with the reader to the last page. Suddenly out of nowhere, come his final words, a tirade against the monks that is dominated by verbal play: "As for their studies, they read only Pantagrueline books not so much to pass time merrily as to hurt some one mischievously. How so? By fouling and befouling, by twiddling their dry fingers and fingering their dry twiddlers, by twisting wry necks, by bumming, arsing and ballocking, by devilscutting, in a word by calumniating. Rapt in this task, they are like nothing so much as the brutish village clods who in the cherry season stir up the ordures of little children to find kernels to sell to druggists for pomander oil" (*P*, 34).

In the final analysis, *Pantagruel* remains a rough schematic work which serves as a trial balloon for Rabelais. It is not a harmonious book in which the themes are well orchestrated. Although it follows in general the pattern of a pseudo epic, it skips along from one disconnected episode to another. Rabelais has not yet mastered the story-telling trade; the tales are not amalgamated with the mainstream of the narrative, as they will be later. He simply aligns one tale with another. Although the episodes dealing with Panurge and his adventures form the highlight of the book, they completely disrupt the structure of *Pantagruel*. Rabelais does not fully develop giganticism with all its comic and thematic possibilities. Even if its presence in the book is much more than perfunctory, its effect remains limited by its simplistic and often crude appearance. Pantagruel adheres largely to the hero whom medieval theater or epic tradition handed down; Rabelais has not considerably enlarged upon the original canvas.

Vulgarity dominates much of the book. Whereas the verve of later works is sufficient to free us from any revulsion we might otherwise have toward their obscenity, the crudity of *Pantagruel* remains harsh and continues therefore a trend found in medieval popular literature. It would be sheer conjecture to state that the first book is an apprentice venture because Rabelais wrote it in a short period of time; no facts could bear out such a statement. Actually the work already contains the Rabelaisian stamp of verbal play and exuberance, satirical exaggeration and deformation, a distorting imagination unwilling to proceed according to a rationally organized plan—all the budding elements of the grotesque. However, in comparison with the forthcoming *Gargantua* where all these components are treated with more originality, *Pantagruel* remains the embryonic effort of a beginner who has greater achievements in store.

CHAPTER 2

Grotesque Achieved and Exceeded

IN many respects *Gargantua,* published in 1534, two years after *Pantagruel,* elaborates on the main themes introduced in the first book: religious satire, parody of the epic, and a dependence on popular tradition and literature; at the same time it goes much beyond the first attempt. In this work Rabelais constructs a universe which is properly his own, using certain props only as a point of departure, after he transposes or transforms them, they have little in common with their origins and stand as independent creations. Rabelais finally masters his medium, the grotesque, and presents a well-constructed work in which the events follow a logical order without losing their picaresque quality. Furthermore, *Gargantua* has a much broader scope than *Pantagruel.* The episodes are now fully developed and Rabelais's verve blossoms forth without restraint.

Basically *Gargantua* contains three main episodes: the birth, youth, and education of the giant; the Picrocholine war, or the exploits of Gargantua; and the abbey of Thélème, which gives the impression of an appendage suspended at the end of the book. Two facetious enigmas encompass the bulk of the book. One is presented at the beginning—"the Antidoted Flummeries" which were found supposedly at the end of a parchment giving Gartantua's genealogy. This first riddle is an extraordinary jumble of words which are quite incomprehensible; Rabelais slyly adds that the fact that vermin had destroyed part of the manuscript hinders its comprehension, although now and then one can extract some meaningful bits. Riddles in form of poems were a fashionable pastime in Rabelais's day; veiled in obscure allegory, they usually conveyed some thought or message pertinent to contemporary ideas. Here he enjoys playing the game himself, but he pokes fun at it by making his enigmatic poems completely meaningless. The other enigma is the "Prophetical Riddle," copied for the most part from a contemporary poet, Mellin de Saint Gelais, has a meaning, according to Gargantua: "What else can it refer to but the maintenance and progress of the divine truth?" (*G*, 57). But another character retorts: "For my part I see nothing but the obscurely worded description of a game of tennis" (*G*, 57). Rabelais toys with the genre and with the reader. What matters, however, is the impact which these two whimsical poems have on the work; being pure fantasy, they propel the narrative into an imaginary concept of time and give it a truly fictitious character.[1]

I *Vulgarity Surpassed*

Instead of continuing with the adventures of Pantagruel and Panurge, as he had promised to do at the end of the first book, Rabelais chooses to deal with Gargantua. This choice was dictated by the immense popularity that Pantagruel's father enjoyed at the time the author set out to write his second book. Between 1532 and 1534, eight *Gargantuine Chronicles* appeared, narrating the giant's various fantastic and humorous exploits. Even before these dates, however, Gargantua belonged to a long oral tradition.[2] Legend claimed that Hercules was among his ancestors and portrayed him as a giant who swallowed ships, who came to the rescue of helpless woodsmen or reapers, who formed rivers with his urinary flow, and whose dish or spoon dropped on his way were the megaliths, mostly found in Brittany. As a matter of fact, his legend survives nowadays in that province.[3]

When Rabelais decided to write again he took advantage of the legend's popularity; he even borrowed some scenes from the *Chronicles*, such as the description of Gargantua's clothes, the giant's mare's destruction of a forest with her tail, the giant's visit to Paris, and his theft of the bells from Notre Dame. At first sight one may have the impression that Rabelais gives in to public demand by choosing Gargantua as his new chief protagonist, but it soon becomes apparent that he adapted the giant, and the tradition surrounding him, to suit his own needs.

In the *Gargantuine Chronicles*, for example, the episode of the giant's mare is treated rather tersely. Rabelais imbues it with new life by means of a detailed description of the action which reproduces rhythmically the movements of the tail and by ending the scene with a facetious etymology. He does not satisfy himself with the barest facts; he transforms them, augments them, and even distorts them if necessary:

For suddenly, when in the heart of the forest the wasps attacked her, she swished her tail and, sweeping all about her, not only felled the stingers but uprooted all the trees. Up and down, right and left, lengthwise and athwart, here and there, over and under, before her and aback, this way and that, she mowed down the woods like so much grass. . . . Gargantua delighted by the spectacle, forebore to boast, merely commenting to his followers: "Je trouve beau ce! I find this pleasant." Whence the pleasant land has been known as Beauce ever since (G, 16).

Following a pattern set in *Pantagruel* and dictated by epic tradition, Rabelais first gives a detailed account of Gargantua's birth, which is much more developed and elaborate than that in the first book. From the very start, we can see how *Pantagruel* served as a model or rough draft for *Gargantua*. As an omen of Gargantua's fantastic feats, Gargamelle (gullet), after an eleven months pregnancy, will give birth to her son through her left ear. Critics have pounced on the grotesque episode and interpreted it as a satire or parody on Christ's birth or, because Rabelais says that nothing is impossible to God, as a Lutheran leaning on the author's part.[4]

What is perhaps more important is that in this episode, Rabelais begins to demonstrate his Renaissance humanism by citing a flood of ancient authorities to prove the authenticity of his claim. The enumeration of many respected sources for such an unusual occurrence is preposterous in itself, but Rabelais makes it much more so by allowing their names to accumulate to an immensely exaggerated level; a new form of a learned grotesque has been attained, as well as a fusion of the popular and erudite which will henceforth pervade Rabelais's works.

If crudity and vulgarity dominate *Pantagruel*, popular tradition and giganticism account for a good portion of *Gargantua*. The etymology of the name Pantagruel has a pseudo-learned flavor, but in the case of Gargantua, whose first words were: "Drink, Drink, Drink" (G, 7), his father declares "Que grand tu as" (*Ibid.*, "How big is your gullet" [G, 7]), and from this utterance the giant supposedly derives his name. The making of his clothes requires a monstrous amount of material; for his doublet "they used eight hundred and thirteen ells of white satin . . . eleven hundred and five and one third ells of the finest white broadcloth were used for the breeches . . ." and his shoes "calling for four hundred and six ells of dazzling blue velvet— were most stylishly slashed by parallel lines; crossed by uniform cylinders. The soles alone required eleven hundred hides of brown cows" (*G*, 8). Rabelais takes great delight in exaggerating beyond the call of duty; he takes us beyond the superhuman into the realm of the fantastic and the inconceivable. He surpasses the exaggerations of the *Chronicles* while at the same time he defines precisely the amount of material needed to one-third of an ell; a comic contrast results from the gigantic number and the superfluous precision. In addition, Rabelais's dwelling on the giant's clothes and physical appearance partly indicates that this book adheres to a facet of the Renaissance spirit: emphasis is given to beautiful dress, jewelry, and to the care of one's outward bearing.

The description of Gargantua's adolescence gives further proof of Rabelais's evolving imagination. In the first book, he emphasizes Pantagruel's strength and crude actions in a rather simple narrative style. In the second book, although Rabelais continues to underline the animalistic life of a newborn child, he has hit upon a stylistic innovation which draws our attention away from the vulgarity. He describes Gargantua's actions by means of proverbs and, to show the helplessness and unconsciousness of the child, he purposely twists and inverts the meaning of the aphorisms. The description of the giant's childhood is accomplished through a huge accumulation of proverbs which goes beyond its descriptive purpose; again Rabelais has found a means of indulging in his favorite game—verbal play: "Gargantua was also inclined to look a gift horse in the mouth . . . tell cock and bull stories . . . throw the helve after the hatchet . . . rob Peter to pay Paul . . . fence in the cuckoo to preserve the summer and keep the moon safe from the wolves . . . hope, if the heavens fell, to catch larks . . . make a virtue of necessity . . . cut his coat according to his cloth . . . split no hair and care as little for the shaven as for the shorn . . ." (*G*, 11).[5]

As part of the description of Gargantua's childhood activities, Rabelais produces an interminable list of games which supposedly help the young giant pass his time. A giant will play more games than a normal child, and therefore the list contains several hundred, many more than are necessary even for Gargantua. Some have held that these lists are tedious, that they stop the flow of the narrative, and that they are totally unnecessary and archaic, although they might have interested Rabelais's contemporaries.[6] One must keep in mind that as a true humanist, Rabelais took great pleasure in displaying his knowledge. In this case, he follows one of the manias of his day: "Another variety of amusements included *Primus Secundus,* which resembled *Tiddlywinks; Mark Knife,* which consisted in tossing a coin as close as possible to a blade buried in the table; *Keys,* like the above save for the use of keys instead of coins; *Shovel Board,* in which three counters or coins were slid over a smooth board; *Odd or Even,* in which the players must guess the number of coins in a closed fist; *Cross and Pile,* sometimes called *Heads or Tails; Knucklebones; Jacks;* and *Ground Billiards* or *Croquet*" (*G*, 22).

Rabelais deems it proper and necessary to picture giganticism both thematically and verbally; the accumulation of words and lists is another form of it. Furthermore, these catalogues of words have an esthetic value in that they acquire a sonorous rhythm through sheer accumulation and often contain an interplay of sounds and meanings; they stand as further evidence of the author's verve and not as obstacles to skip or overcome. To get a vivid picture of Gargantua's pastimes, one should consult Peter Brueghel's (the Elder) paintings, "Children's Games" and "The Netherland's Proverbs." Brueghel's art expresses much of the tone and flavor found in *Gargantua.*

Satire comes to full fruition in *Gargantua* because in it imagination and the grotesque reach a high creative level. The character of the satire will never be surpassed in subsequent books although it will be equaled. In key instances one could say that satire is gratuitous; the episode in which it exists acquires comic and esthetic values which surpass by far the critical or moralizing intent. A case in point occurs in the scenes involving Janotus de Bragmardo, a theologian from the Sorbonne whose vulgar name immediately sets the tone of the ensuing episodes.

[36]

Grotesque Achieved and Exceeded

One of Gargantua's actions upon arriving in Paris is to carry away the bells from Notre Dame. In the popular *Chronicles* this facetious undertaking figures as an independent episode that illustrates the giant's prowess, but Rabelais diminishes its importance and uses it only as the background for his ridicule of the erudition of the Sorbonne scholars. Janotus is sent by his superiors to recover the bells from Gargantua. A vulgar presentation of the theologian is avoided through the use of metaphors and puns which enhance the ridiculous:

Master Janotus, with a haircut like that affected by Julius Caesar, settled the traditional doctoral hood over his cootlike head. Next, he antidoted his stomach against possible contamination, with cakes baked in the most secular ovens, and holy water from his excellently stocked cellar. Then, he proceeded to Gargantua's. Before him crawled three black beadles; behind him he dragged five or six servile and artless Masters of Arts, all of them mildewed and rotten as cheeses (*G*, 18).

Their entrance on stage could not be any more theatrical or farcical and brings out the satire. From the very beginning, we have not dealt with serious characters, and their purpose in being borders on the absurd. They come to reclaim the bells which Gargantua and his companions have already decided to return; therefore Janotus' harangue falls on deaf ears because of its uselessness. The harangue in macaronic Latin, here latinized French, consists of a pastiche of the types of speech made by the sophists: a mixture of French and Latin, with more bad Latin than good French. The deformation occurs through using corrupted Latin with a vulgar intention; the parody becomes obvious when this usage is contrasted with the fact that Latin is a language usually held in high esteem: "By my faith, Domine, by God's body, if you will sup with me *in camera charitatis,* in the guest hall, *nos faciemus bonum cherubin,* we shall make good cheer. *Ego occidi unum porcum,* I have slain a porker, *et ego habet bon vino,* and it's good wine I have, too. But of good wine, man cannot make bad Latin" (*G*, 19).

In Janotus, Rabelais has created a caricature of a theologian, but not à la Daumier. The sophist does not appear in a harsh light; on the contrary he is quite harmless. He appears to be a puppet who acts automatically and unconsciously with no hidden motives; he performs on a burlesque level, according to the criteria set forth by his profession, and therefore he arouses the reader's pity, not scorn. The jargonistic harangue pleasantly distorts the character; it does not serve as a critical but as a mocking device. What dominates the episode is a grotesque concept of Janotus created by his harangue. Although in the end the theologian will discard any so-called altruistic motives in claiming the bells by concerning himself strictly with personal gain, the sordidness of this pathetic greed is still overshadowed, in the final analysis, by this meaningless and would-be pompous address.

II *Fusion of Parody, Satire, and Giganticism*

In keeping with epic tradition, Gargantua's test comes when he is called back by his father Grandgousier to defend his country against Picrochole (bitter bile) and his invading army. It has now been established that Rabelais drew on family history from his native region. His father Antoine, a lawyer, and a neighbor, Gaucher de Sainte-Marthe, had a quarrel that caused a lawsuit concerning fishing rights on the Loire River. Rabelais takes this basic incident and inflates it out of proportion, transforming it into a monumental conflict in which Antoine becomes Grandgousier and Gaucher, Picrochole.[7] To emphasize the pettiness and the stupidity of war, the Picrocholine catastrophe begins when Grandgousier's shepherds ask some of Picrochole's bakers to sell them some cakes, and instead of satisfying the request, the latter beat the poor shepherds for no reason whatsoever. The old and peace-loving Grandgousier, after attempting to avoid bloodshed, finally calls upon his son to right the wrong.

The Picrocholine war, which forms the bulk of *Gargantua* perfectly fuses parody, satire, and giganticism. Episodes anticipating Gulliver's encounter with the Lilliputians abound throughout, and suggest the giant's size in metaphoric terms: "Suddenly a ruffian gunner in the fort fired a cannon ball at him, striking him violently on the right temple. Gargantua was no more hurt than if it had been a grape seed. Indeed he believed it was. 'What is it?' He commented. 'Why are you tossing grape seeds at us? The vintage will cost you dear!' . . . So thick fell the projectiles that Gargantua turned to Ponocrates: Gad, my dear fellow; these flies are blinding me, give me a branch off one of these willows to chase them off" (*G*, 31). The techniques employing giganticism show more sophistication and artistry than in the first book. The concrete images that increase the feeling of awe and unreality are continued. They create an effective contrast between the suggestive huge size of Gargantua and their own insignificant sizes. Rabelais can suddenly bring Gargantua down to human scale by describing him performing human actions, while his huge body continues to loom in the background. Once again the popular strain in the book leads to satire: "While changing his clothes, Gargantua ran through his hair a thousand-foot comb, with teeth made of solid elephant tusks. At every rake he gave, more than seven cannon balls, which had struck there since the battle of Vède, fell crashing to the ground. Seeing this, Grandgousier leaped to the conclusion they were lice. 'Upon my word, son, why have you brought us verminhawks from the Collège of Montaigu? I did not know you had taken up residence there'" (*G*, 37). Rabelais here obliquely attacks the unsanitary conditions which prevailed in the schools under the supervision of the monks, but the satire, being couched in a metaphor, loses some of its moralizing sting.

In the episode involving the pilgrims (*G*, 38), Rabelais uses the same device of adapting the giganticism to be a backdrop for the satire. Popular tradition reigns supreme when Gargantua inadvertently swallows in a lettuce salad the pilgrims who earlier had sought relief from their fatigue in the shadow of the plants. As they are crawling back up, with the help of their distaff, one of them hits a sensitive tooth; irritated, the giant plucks them out individually with a toothpick the size of a tree. Here the grotesque has a creative rather than a rhetorical function. Several chapters later, however, the pilgrims are brought back on stage, and Grandgousier, the wise and rational father, admonishes them in direct terms: "Go your ways in the name of God the creator, and may He guide you forever. Henceforth do not be so ready to undertake these idle and unprofitable journeys. Look after your families, work each at your trade, educate your children and live by the teachings of that good apostle Paul. Do this and you will earn the protection of God, His Angels and His Saints; nor is there plague or evil that can possibly assail you!" (*G*, 45).[8]

When Rabelais deals with a point of view that greatly angers him he clearly states his criticism of it. Such occurrences, however, are not very frequent in Rabelais's works; he prefers to veil his satire, partly because of the sensitive subject matter attacked, but above all because he intends to give more significance to the scene or characters created than to the principles attacked through them. In other words, the episode matters more as an artistic composition than as a vehicle for the author's thought.

In *Pantagruel,* giganticism had its own intrinsic value, that of sheer exaggeration. In *Gargantua,* although we still find it used to stress the immeasurable size and the strength of the giant, it no longer depends solely on this role for its existence. The device has become a basic element in the narrative and serves as an avenue for the expression of a moral or satirical intention. Rabelais no longer imitates the pattern of medieval romances in his use of giganticism as he did in the case of the Werewolf episode. Gargantua goes through only superficial motions, and Friar John, who first appeared at the outbreak of the Picrocholine war, now shares the spotlight with him.

The introduction of Friar John parallels that of Panurge in *Pantagruel.* They both function like a grain of yeast; as soon as one of them appears, the tempo increases. Through them, Rabelais channels much of his verve and gusto. Both are vivacious characters; they constitute a materialization of their creator's cult of energy and movement. The basic difference between the two is that Panurge evolves throughout the books and becomes an individual with whom we can identify, whereas the idealized monk remains a type. Many have tried to find sources for Friar John; in contrast to Panurge's case, the results have been quite inconclusive. As a matter of fact, it makes little difference where Rabelais might have found the prototype for his character because the monk stands on his own merits. Besides being highspirited, his most notable attribute, he embodies the epic parody and the monastic satire.

When we first meet Friar John, he is defending his monastery against Picrochole's hordes. With this character, Rabelais gives us a picture of an antimonk and antitheologian—the opposite of Janotus de Bragmardo. The author fixes Friar John in our minds by means of a masterful portrait that ranges from the physical to the moral and immediately sets the hero in a favorable light, whereas the theologian's portrait abounded in mockery: "At the time, the abbey included a monk called Friar John of the Funnels, a youthful, gay, wide awake, good humored and skillful lad. Tall, slim, with a wide mouth and a great nose, bold, venturesome, deliberate, Friar John was a crack patterer of psalms; he could polish off a mass or get through a vigil in record time. In brief, here was a true monk if there ever was one since the monking world started monkeying in monkeries. Withal, when it came to the breviary, a clerk to the teeth" (*G*, 27).

This portrait pictures an active individual who differs from most of his colleagues.[9] Like many of them, he disposes readily of liturgical and monastic obligations, but he does not idle his free time away. Rabelais derides these idlers by creating a family of words which alliterate denigratingly: "since the monking world started monkeying in monkeries." In the next breath, he praises Friar John who is a biblical expert and "clerk to the teeth." This last image purposely shifts attention from his present condition and announces his forthcoming role. The military image "armed to the teeth" is adapted to a different context in order to determine Friar John's biblical authority and to show where his qualities lie. Actually, the monk does not become heroic to defend the monastery power but to save the productive vineyards which surround it.

Friar John, as the symbol of the ideal monk, focuses the satirical attack against his brethren and their proverbial inactivity and ignorance. Of course these vices are somewhat exaggerated to fit the satirical purposes. Any truly malicious intent disappears, however, when wilful absurdity distorts all logic; this distortion creates a grotesque satire which becomes more grotesque than satirical. Rabelais's typical procedure is to follow an admissible train of thought and then suddenly to introduce a playful or ridiculous element; the trap door flies open and the void swallows the implied seriousness. It is as if, at the right moment, he pulls the rug from under us: "For my part, I study not at all; in our abbey we avoid learning for fear of mumps, our late abbot always said it was a monstrous thing to see a learned monk" (*G*, 39).

By making reference to a medieval tale, Rabelais himself explicitly indicates the presence of parody in the episode that depicts Friar John defending the next year's wine crop: "Maugis the hermit, celebrated in the *Tale of the Four Sons of Aymon,* never acquitted himself more heroically against the Saracens with his pilgrim's crook than Friar John of the Funnels against the pillaging cake-bakers with the staff of the cross" (*G,* 17). Among the monk's prodigious feats, the one which stands out is his killing of thirteen thousand six hundred and twenty-two soldiers; this hyperbole sets the facetious tone for the whole episode. Rabelais might easily have intended to parody the *Song of Roland* and the exploits of Bishop Turpin of Rheims, a fighting companion of Charlemagne's nephew. But what a hierarchical discrepancy between the high ecclesiast and the lowly monk acting for a rather dubious purpose! Roland, like the heroes of antiquity who had their arms forged by Vulcan, possessed a magic sword; his weapon, Durandal, owed its indestructibility to the relics it contained. Friar John, too, has an invincible weapon with divine powers, a distaff of a cross which he will use in the slaughter. What a contrast the sublimity of a divinely enchanted sword and the desecrating use of a religious implement; parody emerges from this confrontation.

In keeping with medieval tales, Rabelais takes great delight in giving detailed physiological descriptions of the slaughter. In this manner, he not only feigns adherence to tradition but also displays his vast medieval knowledge. Although gory details formed an integral part of them, the medieval and epic tales kept such description within reasonable limits. In his constant endeavor to expand events to a gigantic scale, Rabelais takes more than an extra step to inflate Friar John's accomplishments to an unheard of proportion. Placing events on a prodigious level will give them epic proportions, but when the exaggeration removes any semblance of reason or logic, parody sets in. The carnage in which Friar John indulges becomes parody by giving the impression of a small giant knocking down so many puppets; the lack of real emotions or life in the distorted episode allows an impersonal and comic element to assert itself.

Thwack to the right, thwack to the left, Friar John struck in the old-fashioned style of fencing; thwack, thwack, he felled them like so many hogs. He brained some, smashed the legs and arms of others, broke a

[42]

neck here, cracked a rib there. He flattened a nose or knocked an eye out, crushed a jaw or sent thirty two teeth rattling down a bloody gullet. Some had shoulder blades dislocated, others their thighs lamed to pulp, others their hips wrenched, others their arms battered beyond recognition (G, 27).

The Picrocholine war affords Rabelais the opportunity to let his imagination run freely, if not wildly. The battleground, located in his own native region, comprises only a few square miles; yet in this limited area he playfully places hundreds of thousands of soldiers who take part in the most monstrous encounters. If he wishes, Gargantua could straddle the whole field with one step. Hence Rabelais handles giganticism with two different *optiques,* as if he were juggling with it—on the one hand, he expands disproportionately; on the other hand, he brings the giants down to a human level. Gargantua's struggle against Pirochole, does not have the dense and opaque materiality which dominated the Pantagruel *vs.* Werewolf episode; a light fantasy dilutes the events that deal with the size and feats of the giant.

In a way, the Picrocholine war serves as the link, though sometimes a tenuous one, which ties together about two-thirds of the book. From it, evolve side tales such as the one concerning Gymnates, one of Gargantua's companions, who performs extraordinary acrobatics on a horse, as his name indicates he can do, and hoaxes his assailants in order to escape from them; or the short narrative describing Friar's John's escape from his captors. These tales are reminiscent of, and form a counterpart to, Panurge's escapades in the first book, but their esthetic superiority derives from the fact that they are fused to the main narrative of *Gargantua;* whereas Panurge's devilries in *Pantagruel* are simply enumerated with no real thematic anchor to that book. Such an evolution in his techniques of narration proves the maturing of the creative Rabelais; his work has become an artistic enterprise rather than a simple means of enumerating disconnected tales.

The Picrocholine war episode allows Rabelais to express his opinion on war and tyrants.[10] He explicitly rejects war as a means of resolving conflicting interests. Grandgousier stands for the peace-loving monarch who is drawn into a struggle by an overly ambitious dictator. However, if Rabelais simply wanted to show his attitude toward war, he certainly has placed too much emphasis on Picrochole. Because of this emphasis, the character acquires more scope and is transformed into a creation which transcends its apparent role—that of a simple tyrant figure. The stage for the ludicrous is set by the vulgar or ironic names of Picrochole's staff: Rashcalf, Tickledingue, the Duke of Small-title, Count Swashbuckles, Captain Krapp, and Captain Draw-forth (always retreating).

Taken globally, the Picrochole episodes parody the extravagant dreams of a conquering tyrant. The scene that deals specifically with his imaginary conquests is a transposition of Plutarch's portraits of Pyrrhus, but the dialogue between the Persian king and his adviser forms a mere canvas, a point of departure, which Rabelais will amply embroider.[11] To begin with, Rabelais, instead of one, creates a number of counselors who constantly excite and incite Picrochole with temptations of fantastic land conquests; he becomes a toy which they manipulate as they please. In Plutarch, Pyrrhus' ambitions belong to the realm of possibilities (after Italy, he plans to occupy only Sicily and North Africa), but Picrochole's dreams are completely irrational. Pyrrhus retains his self-mastery, but Picrochole shows absolutely no capacity to think realistically. Plutarch implicitly criticizes his character, whereas Rabelais ridicules his absurd creation through his exaggerated dreams:

One part falls upon Grandgousier and his men, routing them at the very outset . . . the other part of Your Majesty's forces will bear upon. . . . In heaven's name, what shall we drink in the desert? We have already provided for everything. . . . Fourteen huge crafts speed across the Syrian Sea laden with the choicest vintages of the world. I see them sailing into Jaffa. There, twenty-two thousand camels and sixteen hundred elephants await them. (You remember, you captured them . . . when you entered Lybia) . . . We shall meet them anon. Already they have conquered Brittany, and Normandy, Flanders. . . . They rally in Bohemia after sacking Swabia. . . . Bravely they march against Lübeck, Norway, Sweden, Denmark . . . (G, 33).

By juggling with verb tenses, Rabelais destroys the barriers of time; the future is telescoped into the present or even the past. Picrochole no longer controls his senses; with one broad jump, he straddles the vast abyss that separates the future from the past, and his imagination soars to great heights. To denigrate his character and show his ignorance, Rabelais, in the midst of all these sublime dreams, has Picrochole show concern for his physical well-being: "In heaven's name what shall we drink in the desert?" It should be noted that the Pyrrhuses, or Picrocholes who appear in more recent literature—in Montaigne, Boileau, or La Fontaine—show Rabelais's influence; they are world conquerors who are not satisfied with limited conquests.[12]

Although the Picrochole episode has a moralizing and imitative purpose, it is not obviously didactic. The conquering clown is simply not aware that his dreams are absurd, coming as they do from an insignificant landlord. The endless enumeration of conquered countries enhances the gratuitousness of the scene and its exaggeration introduces the grotesque element. In order to make this character appear even more worthless, the whole episode is set in a facetious and imaginary concept of time and space; therefore, the end really remains unknown. Picrochole was advised that "his kingdom would be restored to him . . . at the coming of the dodo birds and cocklicranes. . . . No one knows what has become of him. However, I did hear that he is now a common stevedore at Lyons, quite as waspish as ever . . ." (G, 49). If Picrochole had been killed in self-defense, his end might have been heroic. A burlesque exit is necessary to show the fullest scorn for this enemy of peace. In contrast, Gargantua stands out as the enlightened and benevolent victor. Instead of harshly punishing the vanquished, he makes them work the newly installed printing presses; their energies will now be used to spread knowledge.

III *Thélème: Ideal or Fantasy*

The defeat of Picrochole, the subsequent rewards by Gargantua to his soldiers, and his didactic address to the vanquished would form a fitting and logical conclusion to the book, but with a rather artificial transition—"There remained only the monk to provide for"—Rabelais adds on another appendage, the extremely detailed description of the abbey of Thélème (from the Greek "will" or "desire"). Thélème represents an ideal antimonastery, and it lives up to its name by the motto which regulates the lives of its inmates: "Do as thou wilt."

Although, structurally speaking, the abbey of Thélème might appear to be an afterthought, that possibility does not detract from its relevance. In essence, Rabelais describes not a monastery but an idealized Italian Renaissance city-state such as Ferrara or Urbino; he could and must have had in mind Baltazar Castiglione's *Il Cortegiano,* published in 1517, an account of how a courtier should live and what he should strive for. The abbey's motto is not as revolutionary as it first seems; after all, only individuals with the best potential are admitted to it, and honor guides and controls their every thought or action. Consequently, "Do as thou wilt" proceeds naturally from their moral code of behavior; no other would be fitting. One could almost say that Thélème stands as an exemplary type of institution and not as a substitute monastery.

Of course, Rabelais through this abbey sneers at celibacy, at life regulated by the sound of bells and restrained by walled enclosures, and at the many misfits who traditionally peopled these places; but following his usual creative process, he builds an episode that drowns out much of the didacticism.[13] Since utopias and treatises of courtly behavior are fashionable, he will gladly profit from their popularity and incorporate one into his *Gargantua.* Above all, however, such an episode will be another means for his imagination to run rampant, to elaborate and amplify and thereby satisfy his creative urge.

Rabelais has, indeed, some rather harsh words for those who have no honor or goodness and still seek admittance into his abbey: "Here enter not, smug hypocrites or Holy loons,/ Bigots, sham-Abrahams, impostors of the cloth,/Mealy mouthed humbugs, holier-than-thou baboons,/Lip service lubbers, smell feast picaroons . . ." (*G*, 54). The seriousness disappears even here because of the voluminous accumulation of inadmissible characters given in the inscription engraved on the main gate of the monastery, and the playful cacophony that emerges from the listing of epithets.

Furthermore, the dominating elements of the episode consist of elaborate descriptions of the architecture of the building, the accommodations for the monks and nuns, and the apparel worn there. Once the intellectual and moral fiber of the individuals that is implied by their very admission on the premises is taken for granted, the emphasis is placed on their outward appearance and well-being, thereby echoing the description of Gargantua's clothes.

Rabelais basks in extensive descriptions of beautification: "In winter, their gowns were of taffeta in all the colors mentioned above, but lined with lynx, weasel, Calabrian marten, sable and other rare fur. Their beads, rings, chains and necklaces were of precious stones: carbuncles, rubies, balas rubies, diamonds, sapphires, emeralds, turquoises, garnets, agates, beryls and priceless pearls" (G, 56). The building has the shape of a hexagon, perhaps because the circle suggests perfection. From his travels in Italy, Rabelais incorporates into his abbey features of the sumptuous palaces he had seen as well as details from some of the châteaux in the Loire Valley, but his monastery exceeds these other buildings in size and splendor because he always finds it necessary to magnify his creations and place them on an extraordinary plane:

. . . in each corner rose a great circular tower, each identical, sixty yards in diameter. . . . The distance between each tower was three hundred and twelve yards. . . . The building was a hundred times more magnificent than Bonnivet, Chambord or Chantilly . . . There were nine thousand three hundred and thirty-two suites. . . . The steps, grouped in units of twelve between each landing, were of porphyry, of Numidian stone, of serpentine marble . . . at each landing, two splendid round antique archways admitted the light and led to an open loggia . . . (G, 53).

The reader loses himself in a maze of details, so that the rhetorical nature of the episode is rapidly overshadowed by them. Consequently what emerges is the fact that the abbey is a creation of Rabelais's fantasy; the moral takes a minor although still significant role. The descriptive abundance, another form of the grotesque, tips the scale in favor of creative imagination instead of satirical or ethical intent. Structurally speaking, the suspended episode reinforces this esthetic interpretation. By attaching the abbey of Thélème to the end of the narrative, Rabelais again shows his need to take a basically potent embryonic notion and expand it to the bursting point in order to give in to his ebullient fantasy.

Gargantua marks the end of a phase in Rabelais's creative process. Henceforth, he will not use so much popular material. He will not make the feats of the giants the basis of his works; he has sufficiently exploited these topics. He has exercised on these themes and mastered them. His tastes evolved as he reached his artistic maturity; he acquired a reputation as a writer and abandoned certain facile techniques and effects that were appropriate to the central themes of *Pantagruel* and *Gargantua*. From now on he takes advantage of the popularity of other contemporary preoccupations. Some hold that *Gargantua* is Rabelais's masterpiece because of its near-perfect orchestration of satire, parody, and popular elements as well as its fairly cohesive structure, but above all, because of its unusual creative verve. Others maintain for somewhat different reasons that the *Third Book* deserves the supreme accolade of the critics. After the following chapter, the individual reader may make his own choice.

CHAPTER 3

The Socratic Banquet

WITH the publication of the *Third Book,* Rabelais for the first time claims authorship of one of his works, instead of attributing it to Alcofribas Nasier, his anagrammatic pseudonym. His reputation is established firmly now, and as he has the support of the king, François I, he thinks he need no longer fear the Sorbonne's repercussions. Twelve years have elapsed since the appearance of *Gargantua.* When he again sets out to write, Rabelais chooses to use as a backdrop for his book the *Querelle des Femmes* ("The Quarrel of the Women") which pits admirers and critics of women against each other.[1] He brings forth Panurge once more, after his absence from *Gargantua,* and makes him the chief protagonist who seeks throughout the book the answers to the questions: shall I marry? shall I not marry? What strikes one first in this book is its sharp thematic break with two preceding works: no more gigantic feats or parodies of epic or medieval tales. The rather long interlude between books allowed Rabelais to regenerate his subject matter drastically to fit the new exigencies of his artistic and philosophical maturity, and of his times and the new tastes of his readers.

I Structure and Movement

Structurally the *Third Book* parallels *Gargantua* in that the bulk of the work is embraced by two hyperbolic episodes in the form of satirical praise. Panurge starts out by praising debts and the necessity of having them—a startling paradox. However, the praise accumulates to such a disproportionate amount that it soon submerges this topic in ridicule. As a matter of fact there is an imbalance between the means and the end, between the supposed eloquence and the trivial subject which this eloquence seeks to explain; the overabundant rhetoric is purposely unfitting to the cause at stake. Rabelais gives precedence to the form to the detriment of the idea. In his praise of debts, Panurge declaims in order to excuse his prodigality, but unable to control his imagination, he shifts from a personal plane to a universal one.[2] He promotes an impossible Utopia ruled by his own amoral standards. The flow of words unfurls at such a rapid rate that he no longer knows what he is saying; he intoxicates himself with his own sputtering and its cacophony:

Just imagine another world, where all men borrowed and all lent, all were debtors and creditors. Oh, what a harmony would attend the regular motions of the heavens! I think I can hear it as plainly as Plato when, beholding a siren upon each of the eight circles of the planetary system, he listened to the music of the spheres. What a perfect symphony among the elements! How nature would delight in her works and productions! Ceres, laden with corn, Bacchus with wine, Flora with blossoms, Pomono with fruits, and Juno, throning it in the ethereal heights, a model of serenity, health and pleasure. I am lost in this lofty contemplation (III, 4).

Panurge cannot long remain on such a lyrical plane; he rapidly descends into the murky depths of his favorite subject of conversation: sex. This unorthodox ending to the speech causes us to wonder if Panurge might have begun the whole praise in order to end with his usual obsession. The speech of praise takes on a gratuitous character because the outburst of lyricism has a paradoxical and meaningless ending.

If a scholar were looking for the sources of this episode, one could be found in Lucian's *De Parasito,* a treatise on the art of being a parasite, in which the author mocks socratic dialectics, just as Rabelais ridicules scholastic dialectics.[3] One could also look at Francesco Berni's (1497–1535) *Capitolo del debito* (chapter [praise] on debt) or at Erasmus' *Praise of Folly*.[4] Rabelais easily surpasses some of these earlier attempts; his praise rapidly leaves the realm of the plausible to reach gigantic proportions on a burlesque metaphysical level. As an antechamber to the *Third Book,* it throws a spoofing shadow on what follows.

In counterpoint to the praise of debts, Rabelais includes a speech praising Pantagruelion, a variety of hemp which because of its numerous fantastic qualities, becomes Pantagruel's fetish.

Without a doubt this praise has a serious purpose; it has been interpreted, and rightly so, as a hymn to progress, an apology for human industriousness as well as an enigma to be solved by the learned world.[5] The author portrays his sincerity and enthusiasm as he lauds the power of this plant: "How without Pantagruelion, could we ring our churchbells? How cover and protect our windows? From this herb, the priests of Isis and the pastophors, or pontiffs, derive their robes; no human but immediately upon birth is hastily wrapped up in it. Not all the various varieties of laniferous trees, not all the cotton trees of Seres or Tibet, of northern China, or India, of Tylos in the Persian Sea, of Arabia, of Malta—not all of these, added together, clothe as many people as that small herb" (III, 51).

It takes four chapters to describe the qualities of the plant; such an abundance of words is much too disproportionate to the task it purports to undertake. Some of the virtues attributed to the Pantagruelion are most extraordinary: it kills vermin, softens nerves, alleviates gout, rheumatism, and burns, and distends the joints. The whole last chapter discusses its incombustibility. It is true that Rabelais, like Pliny, one of his sources, confuses hemp with asbestos. Has Rabelais blindly imitated his source or does he feign confusion?

By attributing these fantastic virtues to the plant, Rabelais derides his own praise and causes it to lose much of its seriousness. Then to what extent can we believe him? He knows himself that he plays with our credulity: "I have told you great and wonderful things about Pantagruelion; but if, short of taxing your credulity, you will believe another divine virtue of this sacred plant's, I will gladly tell it to you. To be sure, your faith or scepticism is all one to me" (III, 52). By ending the *Third Book* with such excessive praise, Rabelais transmits a certain inconsequence to what precedes. The episode of the Pantagruelion brings to mind the abbey of Thélème in that each breaks the continuity of the narrative—each remains suspended at the end without bearing any relationship to the rest of the book. Encased in excessive praise, the meaning of the main narrative, portraying Panurge in quest of an answer to his questions, becomes doubtful; with the two eulogies as foundations, it cannot rest securely.

The *Third Book* has been compared to Plato's *Banquet* because the Quarrel of Women and the problem of marriage have the same role in it as love does in the socratic banquet, that is to say, both topics are discussed dialectically in the respective works.[6] To obtain an answer to the question whether or not he ought to marry, Panurge sets out to seek answers from all sources of human knowledge, accepted or esoteric: dice, dreams, a sibyl, a deaf-mute, a poet, a so-called scientist, a theologian, a physician, a skeptic philosopher, a judge, and a fool; he also consults Friar John, Epistemon, and Pantagruel. Repeatedly, Panurge gets a negative answer, which he refuses to interpret as such and which he distorts to make positive. The few times he receives an affirmative prognostication, his joy soon fades because he also wants to know if, after the marriage, he runs the risk of being cuckold, and of course no one can reassure him on the matter. This danger throws him right back in a quandary, and he continues to propel himself from one consultation to another.

The nature of these consultations creates a sense of ambivalence and suspension. Nothing is set down definitely. If an attempt is made to isolate or define an idea, an opposite reasoning which completely destroys the preceding argument is also presented. The socratic method, not the question at hand, triumphs throughout the book. Each consultation becomes a playlet in which the protagonists expose contradictory notions; as a result the *Third Book* consists of a juxtaposition of such scenes tied together by Panurge's question. Gone is the orchestrated structure of *Gargantua;* once again Rabelais reverts to the picaresque technique that recalls the eclectic *Pantagruel,* of taking his hero through a succession of adventures. The pro and contra argumentation of the *Third Book* results in a movement of flux and reflux which leaves the scenes hanging helplessly, a condition already suggested by the embracing eulogies. Each confrontation between Panurge and his would-be counselors becomes ludicrous because he will never obtain a satisfactory answer; his unreasonable demands and requirements doom his quest to failure from the very start. Therefore, on an esthetic level, these consultations can easily be viewed as theatrical dialogues created in order to indulge in comic contrasts. They are exercises in semantics.

A pervasive movement in the *Third Book* results from different uses of the same word; one could say that the protagonists, using it as a ball, throw the word at each other interpreting it as they see fit. In one of the very first scenes, Panurge quotes lines from Virgil to help him in his decision:

Foemineo prædæ et spoliorum ardebat amore

He was afire to rob, after the fashion of women.
Theft consumed him like a passion.

"Humph!" said Pantagruel. "This means she will steal from you . . ."
"Nonsense!" Panurge protested. "This line means that my wife will love me with all her heart. Juvenal the satirist, did not lie when he said that woman passionately in love sometimes enjoyed stealing from her lover. But what did she steal? a glove, a spangle, a trifling bauble just to give him the trouble of looking for it. By the same token, the bitter disagreements and petty differences that crop up between husband and wife merely serve their love as diversions and stimuli" (III, 12).

Here Rabelais juggles with the word "steal" by having each character interpret it differently. Pantagruel and Panurge bat it around to suit their own needs. In the same spirit as the praise of debts, Panurge unnecessarily expounds at great length as if he were trying to convince himself of his fallacious interpretation. Meanwhile, Rabelais can indulge himself through his character in profuse story-telling that very often bears little relation to the discussion; Panurge continues to be the incarnation of exuberant and massive verbiage, and his creator finds in him an outlet for his overflowing imagination.

What further characterizes the *Third Book* is the movement which derives from the dialogue form. Because the usual rhythmic pattern comes about from the pro and contra argumentation, the cadence has a rather equal beat. One also notices the movement created by the alternation of question and answer; the beat of the rhythm in this case depends on the length of the question and the answer. A particular technique of dialogue worth noting is the consultation between Panurge and Skeinwinder, the Pyrrhonic philosopher. Panurge presses the advocate of doubt with incessant questions which Skeinwinder answers in a monotone and with complete indifference:

Panurge
. . . Shall I marry, then?

Skeinwinder
Perhaps.

Panurge
Will marriage prosper me?

Skeinwinder
That depends upon the circumstances.

Panurge
If I meet favorable circumstances, shall I be happy?

Skeinwinder
Happy enough!

Panurge
Oh, God! Let's go upstream, against the grain!
If I meet unfavorable circumstances?

Skeinwinder
Then do not blame me.

Panurge
For God's sake, advise me. What must I do?

Skeinwinder
Whatever you will (III, 36).

Skeinwinder fends off the charge. Each character unconsciously obeys his particular obsession or professional tic. Panurge blindly keeps up his questioning while the other mechanically answers according to the precepts of his philosophy of doubt. They behave as robots would; their paths never cross.[7] The dialogue becomes a variation on the theme of "shall I marry?" and "I don't know." Because of the wilful redundancy, the words lose expressive value and the dialogue no longer has its usual purpose of question and answer. The movement of this kind of dialogue is composed of a higher and lower pitch than usual directly related to the pressing question and the continuous monotonous answer.

II *From Satire to Verve*

Medicine and law, the two professions traditionally attacked, illustrate Rabelais's techniques of satire. The episode of Judge Bridlegoose whom Panurge never gets a chance to consult is told principally for satirical and narrative purposes. When asked how he passes judgment, Bridlegoose answers: "The dice of sentences and judgments, or, in Latin, *alea judiciorum,* the hazards of decision . . ." (III, 39). All his life he has taken literally the proverbial dictum. Of course, he would not think of changing now. As with Janotus of Bragmardo, the poor judge is not aware of his stupidity; for this reason Pantagruel willingly forgives him his past, and so do we. Bridlegoose continues to base his sentences on legal documents pro forma as well as on the toss of the dice. He follows two opposite paths that will never converge. He defends his decisions by quoting legal codes or proverbs:

I do this as any good judge should, in conformance with *no Spec. de ordinario, III, et tit. de off. om. ju., fl., et de rescriptis praesenta. I,* as Speculator, or Guillaume Durand, indicates in his repertory of canon law.

On the end of the table in my chambers, I place all the bags containing the defendant's plea, and I allow him the first hazard of the dice, just as you gentlemen do, according to *et est not., Favorabiliores, ff. de reg. jur., et in c. cum sunt eod. tit. lib. VI,* which says: *cum sunt partium jura obscura, reo favendum est potius quam actori,* when the law is obscure, the defendant is to be favored rather than the plaintiff (III, 39).

Rabelais caricatures the judges by means of a deformation of professional traits: he misuses judicial procedures and jargon. As a matter of fact, the outlandish accumulation of citations loses all meaning; just as Panurge rises to inflated ethereal heights in his praise of debtors, Bridlegoose does not hesitate through an equally enthusiastic verbiage to exhibit his judicial knowledge. The longer the allusion or quotation, the greater its absurdity and uselessness. With the over-abundance of legal verbiage, Rabelais succeeds in drawing our attention to a grotesquely created character rather than to the implied satire.[8]

To show the difficulty and length of trials, Rabelais adopts an image which is so expanded that it takes on its own individuality: "A suit at its birth seems to me . . . formless and imperfect. A bear newborn, has neither feet, nor hands, nor skin, nor hair, nor head; by dint of maternal licking, it attains perfection in all its limbs. See *no. doct., ff. ad leg. Aquil., I. II, in fi.* Similarly, like yourselves, gentlemen, I attend the birth of a lawsuit. To begin with, it is shapeless, and without distinct limbs. It consists of but one or two documents; it is, in this state, an ugly beast. But heap writ upon writ, pack and pile, brief upon brief, and your lawsuit may be termed full-sinewed and well-boned . . ." (III, 42). Here is Rabelais as an artistic creator who presents an abstract notion concretely and through metaphor underscores the judge's deformation. The author shows himself in the same light when Bridlegoose, to further his argument, tells the story of Perrin Dandin (Tom Noddy) and his son Tenot (Steve) who took on a suit only when it had ripened to a certain point and was ready to pluck, that is, when the outcome was no longer in doubt. But the tale acquires intrinsic value because of the quaint dialogue, the innumerable citations and the precise and pungent characterization, and its moral remains in the background. In such instances, satire forms an incidental canvas for the elaboration of independent episodes. Although much of Rabelais's satire falls into this category, some notable exceptions occur.

The episode in which Panurge seeks advice from Rondibilis the physician sheds light on a more direct and serious technique of satire. After receiving Rondibilis' services, "Panurge without a word, pressed four gold pieces into his palm. Rondibilis accepted them graciously. Then with a start, as though vexed 'Heh Sir!' the physician exclaimed. 'You need not have given me this. Nevertheless, I thank you. I accept nothing of evil folks; I refuse nothing of goodly folk. I am at your service.'—'Provided I pay?' said Panurge.—'Naturally,' the physician answered" (III, 34). Boldly Rabelais aims his criticism at the physician's rapacity; the attack is not veiled by any verbal or caricatural distortion that might considerably reduce the didactic impact. It reminds one of Gargantua's indentical overt approach to pilgrimages. When some fault of society or human vice really irks Rabelais, he indicates his violent reaction to it by explicitly stating his feelings.

Although the Rondibilis episode is found at the end of a chapter, this vehemence has to be ferreted out because the bulk of the consultation deals with the doctor's earthy lecture on sex education and his invective on women.

Indeed, Rondibilis' negative opinions have attracted most of the critics' attention: "When Rondibilis spoke of womankind, he spoke of a frail, variable, capricious, inconstant and imperfect sex. Indeed, with all due honor and respect to Nature, Rondibilis believed that Nature took leave of her senses when she created woman. Surely woman was not fashioned according to the sound principles of common sense, which governed Nature's other creations?" (III, 32). Some ascertain evidence of Rabelais's supposed antifeminism in this passage, and cast him in the camp of the women downgraders during the Quarrel. One must bear in mind, however, that Rondibilis here expresses a biased personal opinion, not necessarily Rabelais's. One has only to look at Panurge's preceding consultations with the theologian Hippothadeus to find woman described as a helpmeet, in accordance with the Bible,[9] and a quick glance at the abbey of Thélème will discover a very enlightened and praising evaluation of woman's intelligence and capacity. Rabelais cannot be forced to one position because he does not have a permanent opinion, as we shall see subsequently; his mind gathers and assimilates but does not fix or systematize.

Some of the episodes have a very tenuous connection with Panurge's quest because most of them are outlets for Rabelais's verbal ebullience and fantasy. Here he abandons all serious pretensions and lets his creative imagination flow freely. Such instances demonstrate the sheer pleasure that he took in the manipulation of words for their sounds, suggestive power, and metaphorical value, or in the grotesque universe which the unrestrained accumulation of them could produce. One could take Panurge's consultation with Herr Trippa, the occultist, as a prime example. In this instance Rabelais has an opportunity to exhibit his knowledge of the occult sciences, but the over-all effect is achieved by accumulation of cabalistic methods of divination which just about become meaningless because of the exaggerated enumeration and acquire above all a sonorous value due to their general pedantic sound and the repeated suffix "ancy": "Herr Trippa then asked Panurge whether he cared to learn the truth

more fully, through pyromancy, or divination by fire? Through
aeromancy, or divination by climatic conditions. . . . Through
hydromancy, or divination by water? Through lecanomancy (an
Assyrian variation of hydromancy) . . . . There was also catop-
tromancy . . . a science founded upon divination by means of
mirrors . . . coscinomancy, or divination by a sieve . . . aleuro-
mancy, or mixing wheat with flour . . . astragalomancy, the science of divination by small bone or dice . . . would you use
tyromancy, or divination by cheese . . . ?" (III, 25). After numerous other suggestions, Herr Trippa asks Panurge: "What is
yours, by the way?—Chewturd, said Panurge" (III, 25). Suddenly, the whole supercilious verbal edifice collapses, since its
usefulness as a meaningful scientific exposition is denied by the
vulgar retort; its gratuitous quality emerges from the chaos of
learned words.

This outburst of verve is not the last, for Rabelais in the very
next chapter overwhelms us with another prodigious verbal display as Panurge seeks Friar John's counsel. It is understandable
that a lively scene ensues since these two characters are the em-
bodiment of physical and imaginative energy. In beseeching
the friar to help him, Panurge, addressing him as "cod," strings
together a series of epithets qualifying the noun: "O dumpy cod,
stumpy cod, famous in birth, famous in girth; O cod, rich in
lactary secretions and heavy as lead; O cod, rose-red; O cod,
above all things fair . . . O tuck, O cod, O stucco cod; O cod
grotesque . . . cod humoresque, cod arabesque . . . O cod,
trussed to be cooked; O cod, cooked to be trussed; O antic cod,
O frantic cod; O mangled, brangled cod . . . O cod positive,
gerundive, genetive and active . . ." (III, 26).

The foregoing catalogue of epithets has a cathartic effect on
Panurge; he is so embittered by Herr Tripps's meaningless consultation that this verbal outburst partially cleanses him of his
frustrations. This enumeration is an extravagant example of the
workings of Rabelais's imagination and therefore has intrinsic
value. The adjectives occur in sonorous parallelisms and contrasting and synonymous meaning. If they appear to have no
congruous relationship to the qualifying noun, they have a metaphorical one; namely, they become images through being transposed from their usual level of meaning into another one. Such

enumerations contain a universe of their own in which the words themselves figure as the characters with lives of their own. They detach themselves from the real world of meaning and reach toward the realm of symbolism.

A final instance of verbal fantasy in the *Third Book* occurs when Panurge consults with Triboulet, the fool. Here, in addition to achieving the effects noted above, Rabelais introduces a variation in the technique. Pantagruel and Panurge cast alternately laudatory or derisive epithets at the fool using contrasting meanings for qualifying adjectives: "An august fool; a very Caesar among fools; a fool imperial, royal, patriarchal, original, loyal, ducal, feudal, seignorial, palatine, principal, praetorian and total," said Pantagruel. Panurge replied: "A fool original and noble, a very pope among fools; a fool consistorian, conclavist, bullist, synodal, episcopal, doctoral, monachal, fiscal, extravagant, a fool of the first tonsure . . . a diapason of fool," said Pantagruel, melodious and full of harmony . . . A caparisonal fool," said Panurge, "malodorous and full of hominy." (III, 38).

Rabelais cannot claim paternity of these catalogues of epithets; he had encountered them in the medieval farces or *soties*.[10] There too the anonymous playwrights had used these devices to create puns on meanings and sounds. In the earlier plays the enumerations had a somewhat plausible appearance, but Rabelais, typically so, constructs a monument of appellations. Whatever he borrows is changed by his distorting imagination. He does not imitate but adapts the source, material, or technique to his own creative purposes.

III *Narrative Techniques: Scholarship and Story-Telling*

In the *Third Book,* Rabelais shows himself in a different light, both as a scholar and a storyteller. In *Pantagruel,* and even to some extent in *Gargantua,* when he told a tale, plausible or not, he did not make much effort to substantiate its veracity: "Now if you don't believe me—'No, truly I do not,' quoth she, to cite a popular song" (*P*, 1). Such feigned protests fit in with the popular character of the early works. A notable exception appears in the description of Gargantua's birth and indicates a transition. Here Rabelais fuses the popular device with a reliance on the ancients and scholarship; among other sources, he counsels: "Read his [Pliny's] *Natural History,* Book VII, chapter III yourselves, and do not plague me farther with the subject" (*G,* 6). Beginning with the *Third Book,* however, he more and more exhibits his self-taught erudition, which is derived from glossaries and adages. One begins to think that every assertion he or his characters make has to be proven either from the ancients or their mythology. Because of the abundance and superfluity of scholarly allegations, the whole procedure gives the impression of a game, perhaps a pastiche from his fellow humanists. To encourage Panurge to seek advice in dreams, Pantagruel admonishes him to:

consider the authorities: Hippocrates in his book *Peri Enuption* or *Of Dreams* . . . Plato in the ninth book of his *Republic* . . . Plotinus, Iamblicus, also a Platonist; Synesius of Cyrene, Bishop of Ptolemius, a fifth-century philosopher and chief authority of Cornelius Agrippa . . . Aristotle, Xenophon, and Galen, in his *Muscular Movement* . . . Plutarch, on the dubiety of autumnal dreaming . . . Artemidorus of Daldis . . . Herophilus, the Bithynian, who was first to dissect the human body . . . Quintus of Smyrna, the fourth-century Greek poet, called Calaber, because his works were recently discovered in Calabria . . . Theocritus . . . Pliny in his *Natural History* . . . Athenaeus and a host of others (III, 13).

Of course, the value of these allusions to authority depends on the seriousness of the matter that they attempt to substantiate. If they pretend to prove some absurd fact, their gratuitousness is self-evident. On the contrary, if they deal with a serious argument, one better tolerates their abundant presence.

With one exception, the racy but whimsical tale of the lion, the fox, and the old lady (*P,* 15), the stories in the first two books are fairly well joined to the main narrative; they form an integral part of the plot. We have only to think of Panurge's escape from the Turks (*P,* 14) or the pilgrims eaten in a salad (*G,* 38). As pointed out, however, the integration of tales in the main body of narrative succeeds better in *Pantagruel* than *Gargantua.* But beginning with the *Third Book* and continuing into the *Fourth Book,* Rabelais not only changes his technique but also introduces more and more tales.[11]

The stories in the *Third Book* are not fused with the episodes in which they are found. Only a tenuous thread keeps them tied to the action of the book. Usually they are told on the pretext of proving a fact or an assertion; on the surface they seem to have a didactic purpose. To illustrate a way to keep a wife faithful, Friar John relates to Panurge the story of Hans Carvel and his ring (III, 28). Ponocrates, one of Gargantua's companions who reappears in this book, narrates the tale of the pope and the nuns to prove that women have curiosity (III, 34). Pantagruel convinces Panurge to seek advice from a fool by giving him an example of a fool's adventures at a roast shop (III, 37). But Rabelais makes these stories break away from their moralizing bounds by infusing them with a life of their own; he accomplishes this with keen characterization in a short space, lively dialogues and concrete details that locate the protagonists in a background known to the readers.

In addition to the tale of Perrin Dandin, already noted, Judge Bridlegoose cites the case of the Gascon soldier who lost money gambling, to substantiate his assertion that sleep is salutary to reaching a decision in legal matters. Before he accepts the case he requires his prospective plaintiff to present him with a sleep certificate, proof that the defendant has arrived at his decision after calm reasoning. The Gascon in his tale, after losing his money at dice, angrily challenges anyone to fight him, but by the time a challenger appears he has placed his loss in a proper perspective. His anger gone after a nap, he invites the imprudent soldier to join in sleep; the fight can wait for later. Although reminded, the reader soon forgets the purpose of the tale: "It was sleep, Bridlegoose wound up, which accomplished the miracle . . ." (III, 42). One remembers instead the animated narration. First Rabelais identifies the hero and his setting: "A certain Gascon in camp at Stockholm; Gratianauld, the fellow was called; he hailed from St. Sever" (III, 42). This distant location, an exotic one for Rabelais's contemporaries, gives the tale an air of fantasy. In presenting it, Rabelais adopts a technique which he often uses: opposing, or fusing, the vulgar and the sublime.

In a scene reminiscent of Panurge's first encounter with Pantagruel, the author creates a contrast between the adventurer's lowly Gascon and German dialects, and Bridlegoose's learned citations of Latin commentaries ranging from Juvenal to medieval jurists. Having gambled away all his pay, the soldier was furious, for:

. . . *pecunia est alter sanguis*, money is a man's very blood by Anto. de Butrio in *c. accedens. ij, extra ut lit. non contest* . . . The gambling ended, Gratianauld then said loudly: Pao cap de bious, hillots, que mau de pippe bou tresbire . . . (God's head, my hearties, may the blindest drunkeness ever distilled in barrel knock you over!) . . . he passed to the camp of the hundred pounders [heavy] or German lanquenets . . . inviting them to combat . . . Der Gascongner thut sich ausz mit eim jeden zu schlagen (The Gascon makes as if to fight everybody) . . . suddenly a French freelancer, who had lost all his money too, determined to fight with the Gascon.

> Ploratur lachrymis amissa pecunia veris,
> (With genuine tears, he wept his vanished cash)

Bridlegoose here cited *Glos de poenitent. distinct 3. c. sunt plures*. (III, 42).

The pungency of the dialogue enhances the dominating flavor of this narration which owes its uniqueness to the cacophonous mixture of various languages.

Rabelais does not confine his short stories to mere narration; on the contrary, in his hands they become animated although in the source material, they are usually blurred. Nor can he claim authorship of most of them, for the greater part are drawn either from Italian writers or from medieval and local tradition.[12] The basic plot for the Gascon warrior comes from Aretino, Hans Carvel and his ring from Poggio Fiorentino, Perrin Dandin, probably from local sources, and the roast shop and the coin tale can be found in so many works that one might assume it belongs to European folklore.[13] As is his custom, Rabelais enlarges the basic elements of these tales by infusing them with his own creative verve. In addition to the methods already mentioned, he enlivens the tales by giving each a perspective or second dimension, mentioning it in a consultation which itself forms a narrative entity. As a result of the frequency of this new genre, the short story, one wonders what caused this innovation in narrative technique.

It seems that between *Gargantua* and the *Third Book*, Rabelais's art matured. He acquired mastery in story-telling and was no longer limited by the general flow of the narrative. His reputation established, he could proceed more freely and with less orthodoxy in his works. He obeys the dictates of his verve rather than the demands of the plot. If he chooses to tell a story, he does not hesitate to digress as long as he pleases because, being an artist, he goes where his imagination takes him. In a sense, the short stories serve the same purpose as the giants and the exaggerations of the earlier books; they are the seeds which his verve fertilizes or fantasies which his imagination inflates.

IV   *The Changing Third Book*

In the last thirty years, especially the last ten, the interpretation of the *Third Book* has undergone profound changes. Traditionally it was agreed that Rabelais interested himself in the Quarrel of Women and composed the book to enter the fray.[14] To prove his antifeminism, the Rondibilis episode is cited, as well as the deft and cold way he has of getting rid of Pantagruel's and Gargantua's mothers: "Indeed the *Supplementum Supplementi Chronicarum* or *Commentary on the Commentary of the Chronicles* [fictitious] states that Gargamelle [Gargantua's mother] died then of sheer joy. For my part, I know nothing about it and care less for her or for any other female" (*G*, 37). To what extent is Rondibilis Rabelais's mouthpiece? One also notes that there are few women in his works. In instances where Rabelais does show a negative attitude toward women, he adheres more to the spirit of popular tradition for its comic effects than to his own feelings. The opposite positive attitude, as we have seen, can also be found in his works. As always, he refuses to restrict himself to any given position; in regard to women, he expresses the traditional ambivalent attitude toward them.

Lately the meaning of the *Third Book* has been questioned further. Rabelais concerns himself not only with the Quarrel but also with the problem of individual marriage.[15] Seen in this light the book becomes an inquiry about marriage, its feasibility and dangers. But it is much more; some see it, and perhaps rightly so, as an inquiry per se, a seeking for counsel rather than a discussion of women and marriage, as a study of Panurge's search for happiness and the impossibility of its success. In this view Rabelais shows the uselessness of a search for moral truth in the established and accepted framework of human knowledge.[16] The solution to the problem lies in oneself rather than in outside sources.

The *Third Book* takes on a socratic meaning; it is not about love or marriage but wisdom. Like Socrates at the Delphi oracle, Panurge seeks to solve the riddle of truth, but he finds only ignorance. In such an interpretation, the emphasis shifts to Hippothadeus, the theologian, who represents divine grace; Rondibilis, nature; and Skeinwinder, reason-doubt. Since these sources prove unsatisfactory, Panurge turns to the wise fools, Triboulet and Bridlegoose as a last resort. Triboulet is a true fool because he has abandoned self-concern. Panurge cannot accept folly in this sense, for he is full of "philautie" or self-love. The answer lies in having faith in God; a belief based on a progressive evangelical ethical system mostly derived from St. Paul, hence quite reformist.[17]

The *Third Book* lends itself beautifully to various interpretations. Of all of Rabelais's books, it has the most philosophical line of thought which can be readily detached from the background of the Quarrel of Women. Basically it appears to be an individual search for truth, wisdom, and happiness. The religious orientation may cause one to raise his eyebrows, because such views possibly contain some inner distortion and prevail at the expense of the artistic creation, which, under ideological lenses, is paid only lip-service. The reader must synthesize various comments in order not to fall prey to any particularly inviting proposition.

CHAPTER 4

Imagination Unbound and the Fantastic

IN the *Fourth Book*, though dealing with the same basic characters, Rabelais infuses new life into his subject and launches his
heroes on a new series of adventures. Since his contemporaries
showed interest in travels and the discovery of new lands, he takes
Pantagruel through imaginary lands in quest of the oracle of the
Holy Bottle which is supposed to give Panurge the final answer to
the questions he posed in the *Third Book*.[1] This is the only link
between the two books; no other theme ties them together. In the
six years (1546–52) that separate the incomplete *Third Book* from
the *Fourth Book*, disregarding the partial edition of the latter in
1548, Rabelais matured further. This last work represents a fusion
and evolution of many of the earlier techniques and preoccupations.

I Artistry in Themes and Structure

Thematically and structurally a certain dichotomy exists between the *Fourth Book* and the earlier works. The construction of
the *Fourth Book* is similar to the *Third Book* in that it consists of
numerous independent episodes which have little bearing on the
quest of the oracle of the Holy Bottle. In fact, this search has even
less relevance to the surrounding episodes than the Quarrel of
Women has in the *Third Book*. In the *Fourth Book*, Rabelais needs
little pretext to enumerate the successive peregrinations of his
characters; he prefers to satisfy his creative urge rather than compose a coherent and well balanced work. In the *Third Book*, his
imagination operates within a limited space, namely that of a
given colloquium with its play upon rhetoric; whereas in the
Fourth Book it is unleashed and spans oceans and fictitious lands
peopled with fantastic creations suggestive of the painter Bosch or
of Disneyland.

Just as the *Third Book* counterbalances *Gargantua* in the structure of the beginning and the end, the *Fourth Book* evokes *Pantagruel* with its vulgar and inconsequential ending. Rabelais ends these latter works very abruptly because to do so fits his over-all jesting scheme; he opens the trap door one final time with this kind of vulgar ending. With the same stroke, he indulges in a last attempt to use a technique derived from popular tradition, which had virtually disappeared. There are few references, for example, to Pantagruel's size: "Shortly after we noticed dropping from his eyes, tears fat as ostrich eggs" (IV, 28). If Rabelais can be accused of using obscene language at the end of the *Fourth Book,* he easily and deftly redeems himself by infusing this vulgarity into the midst of verbal fantasy. After being scared by cannon shots to a very embarrassing extent, Panurge exclaims as the book comes to a close: "Oh, ho, ho, ho, ho! What the devil is this? . . . Do you call this ordure, ejection, excrement, evacuation, *dejecta*, fecal matter, *egesta, copros, scatos,* dung, crap, turds? Not at all, not at all: it is but the fruit of the shittim tree. Selah! let us drink!" (IV, 67).

In the general perspective of Rabelais's works, the *Third Book* forms an interlude which the *Fourth Book* disrupts. Parody of the ancient epic and the medieval tale, so basic to the earlier works, reappears but in a much more veiled fashion than before. Religious satire, done obliquely in the previous book, comes to the fore but rarely overshadows the fantasy in a given episode. Satire of the legal profession does not measure up to the grotesque Bridlegoose scene, but a certain refinement emanates from the new approach. Basically, however, Rabelais does not depart from what he has mastered in the *Third Book;* Panurge's consultations have counterparts in the various visits to strange lands by Pantagruel and his friends. Satire, parody, or didacticism hereafter remain subordinate to Rabelais's continued urge for story-telling, to his creation of a new universe inhabited by fantastic, "surrealistic" creatures, and to his boundless imagination and verbal display.

In composing the *Fourth Book,* Rabelais establishes a playful and ironic relationship between the names of the fictitious lands and the characters who inhabit them. To explain his verbal inventions he adds a glossary at the end of the book which he calls

"Brief Declaration." On their first stop, Pantagruel and his companions land at the Island of Medancothy ("nowhere" in Greek) whose king is Philophanes (eager to see and to be seen). To better describe Shrovetide, he lives on Sneaks Island. The feeble Chitterlings reside on Wild Island. King Panigon (hearty baker) lives on the island of Cheli (roasted meat). King Macrobius (who has a long life) rules the island of the Macreons (people who have long lives). Rabelais also likes to present episodes in contrasting groups; Shrovetide and the Chitterlings, Papemanes (pope adorers) and popefiggers (pope haters), Physis (Nature) and Antiphysis. Rabelais cannot claim originality for many of these episodes; Physis and Antiphysis, for example, come from a contemporary Italian Celio Caliagnini,[2] and the conflict between observers and nonobservers of Lent belongs to folklore.[3] Such episodes as the one dealing with the names of winds on Ruasch Island (windy) or the death of the giant Widenostrils, Swallower of windmills, or the fight with the Chitterlings originate in the *Disciple of Pantagruel,* an anonymous work published in 1537. But as usual, Rabelais draws only on the skeletal framework; when he incorporates a borrowed scene into his work, he expands and transforms it to such a degree that it bears little resemblance to the source.

Two of the best illustrations of Rabelais's ability to transform borrowings are found in the bargaining episode between Panurge and the sheep-dealer Dindenault (Dingdong) at the beginning of the *Fourth Book* and the presentation of Master Gaster at the end. In a way these highly whimsical scenes embracing the book further illustrate the author's two facets: one is earthy whereas the other pretends to convey an erudite moral feeling. Rabelais borrowed the episode between Panurge and Dingdong from Folengo's *Baldus.*[4] In the Italian version, the incident is narrated concisely and tersely without any dialogue. Cingar, one of Panurge's literary ancestors, buys some sheep while on a journey, and to spite the dealer who had abused him, throws the leader of the sheep into the ocean, causing all the other sheep to follow suit. These elements are the basis of Rabelais's version, but what took only a few lines in Folengo occupies several chapters in Rabelais. Folengo's version does not have the bargaining dialogue or Dingdong's praise of the sheep to convince the buyer, which add another dimension to the French version. The features lacking in Folengo show Rabelais's art and give movement and life to the narrative; they form an animated scene which, although it rests on sheer fantasy, puts two characters on stage and gives acute psychological insights into their behavior:

P. I am at your service.
D. You are going to Lanternland, eh?
P. Ay!
D. You are touring to see the world?
P. Ay, truly, truly.
D. And to amuse yourself?
P. Ay truly.
D. I believe your name is Robin Mutton?
P. It is your pleasure to call me so, truly!
D. You are not offended, I trust?
P. Not as I understand, truly.
D. You are, I take it, the king's jester, the king's fool?
P. Ay, truly, truly (IV, 6).

In a dialogue recalling the one between Panurge and Skeinwinder, the Pyrrhonic philosopher with suspended judgment, Rabelais portrays a sly and hypocritical Panurge and a boastful and arrogant Dingdong. In other words, the dialogue serves as a means of caricature and derision.

To further ridicule the character of Dingdong, Rabelais adopts the satirical eulogy which he had masterfully executed in the *Third Book* in the praise of the debtors and the episode of the Pantagruelion. Here the sheep-dealer launches a disproportionate advertisement of his product. He elevates his animals to ethereal heights, so that Panurge will derive more pleasure from bringing them down to a mundane level by throwing them into the sea. Furthermore, the praise falls on deaf ears; it is all the more superfluous because Panurge has already made up his mind as to what he will do. Meanwhile his recurring watchword "patience" shields Panurge from the high-pressure salesman. The situation reminds one of Bragmardo's useless harangue before Gargantua. To show his character in a scornful light, Rabelais has Dingdong distort the facts or use a language much too learned for a man of his position.[5] The dealer is intoxicated with his own verbal deluge just as Panurge was by his praise of the debtors. One feels that Rabelais must have witnessed such a bargaining session at some country fair, but he injects a massive breath of exaggeration into it by means of an avalanche of praise:

These sheep spring of the race of the golden ram who bore Helle and her brother Phryxus through the air, as they fled from Ino, her tyrannous mother-in-law. Poor Helle fell into the sea, which ever since was called Hellespont . . . if you were a scholar, you would know that in the most inferior members of my divine animals (that is, the feet!) there is a bone (that is the heel or the astragal, if you prefer), with which the ancient races used to play at the royal game of *tales* or dice. The only other beast whose heels served thus were the Indian ass and the gazelle of Lybia . . ." (IV, 7).

The last fully developed episode of the *Fourth Book* finds Pantagruel) and his friends visiting Master Gaster (stomach, belly) a personification and symbol of human appetite, whose subjects, the Gastrolators, worship him as their God. The thesis of this action is that man concerns himself more with his physical appetites than with his spiritual needs; and that satisfying the demands of the stomach makes the world go around. Such a notion shows no originality; one of the first examples can be found in Persus, the Latin satirical poet.

The theme of the omnipotence of appetite also appears in a major Spanish work of the fifteenth century, *La Celestina*, which had been translated into French in 1527; Rabelais might have known it through this translation. In addition to its literary origins, the theme certainly must have belonged to common tradition in what was then a predominantly undernourished world. Based fundamentally on the meaning of Master Gaster, interpretations of the episode have varied. For some, the episode represents a sensible and even profound philosophy: the idea of satisfying one's physical needs, of historical materialism; others see in it proof that the body plays an integral part in the spiritual life which gives man his nobility. Finally, it is viewed as a satire on Marsilio Ficino, a fifteenth-century platonic philosopher, who believed that love constitutes man's driving force; in this episode, material necessities are substituted for love.[6] Without a doubt,

Rabelais has a basic message to convey, and one can choose whatever interpretation one prefers, Rabelais could have expounded his thesis in less than six chapters; the difference can be accounted for by the creative process.

When Rabelais does not highly esteem one of his characters, he sketches a short but pungent portrait, as in the case of Master Gaster: "For he is imperious, severe, round, hard, difficult and inflexible" (IV, 57). All the adjectives but one give a moral or behavioral description; however, the exception "round," which evokes his dubious physical appearance, also contrasts with the abstract adjectives and allows the portrait to slip into a lower level of seriousness. Thus Rabelais indicates his derision of Master Gaster.

To substantiate the vulgarization of Master Gaster, the inventions attributed to him are grossly exaggerated. At first he is credited with plausible inventions, showing how he causes civilization to progress and to regress, but suddenly Rabelais blatantly states: "Such was not the limit of Gaster's ingenuity. By a system he discovered, bullets were made to fly backwards, recoiling up on their senders with their original fury, danger and range" (IV, 62). Then he goes on to substantiate the assertion by giving examples of many other irrelevant and unusual life-saving techniques or products. In the unlimited number of extraordinary inventions, we have another satirical eulogy, comparable to the praise of sheep, which gradually shifts to the ridiculous and derides the individual involved. Furthermore, this episode allows Rabelais to burst forth once again with his verbal energy; he devotes two whole chapters to the enumeration of foods which the Gastrolaters sacrifice to their god on both feasting and fasting days: "Next they poured into his mouth the following fare: shoulder of mutton with garlic, meat pies with hot sauce, pork chops with onion sauce, roast capons basted in their own dripping, spring capon . . . goose, kid, fawn and deer, hare and leveret, partridge and choice young partridges, pheasants and delicate young pheasants, peacocks and toothsome young peacocks . . . also cullet fish, sea goose or dolphin, sole, flatfish, mussels, lobster, shrimps, dace, ablet, tench, grayling, haddock, cattlefish . . ." (IV, 59, 60). The author's verbal fantasy achieves in such instances an overwhelming predominance over the didactic or philosophical theme. The prevalence of such artistry not only illustrates Rabelais's superiority over others who have treated the same basic theme but also tends to tilt the balance of interpretation toward an esthetic appreciation instead of an ideological evaluation.

II *Epic Tradition Revisited*

Taken as a whole the *Fourth Book* parodies the epic and the literature of imaginary voyages. Pantagruel and his companions set out on a series of wanderings just as Ulysses and Aeneas had done; these peregrinations give a picaresque flavor to the book. Whereas *Gargantua* refines the theme of the giants and the crudity of *Pantagruel*, the *Fourth Book* shows a purification of the subjects for parody treated in the first book. Rabelais transfigures the real world in the *Fourth Book;* he formulates concrete abstractions and transforms men into animals or objects which cease to be recognizable. In other words, he creates a universe of fantasy which is related to the real world. Each episode takes on the appearance of allegory or myth. Ordinarily myths idealize human life; they are a means of evading the drabness of earthly life by elevating man to a divine level. Because of the boundless grotesqueness and the fantastic setting in imaginary time and space which pervade the book, the allusions to myths do not evoke primarily metaphysical, didactic, or rational meanings in the reader's mind; they stand on their own merit, and the elements of parody remain a distant echo.

The episode of the Chitterlings' fight with Shrovetide finds a counterpart in the scene between Werewolf and Pantagruel in the first book. The first trace of parody appears when Rabelais alludes to the *Iliad* in a burlesque fashion: the Chitterlings will try to deceive the enemy by hiding in a huge sow to be used as a siege engine. Thereby the so-called peers of the Trojans are abruptly brought down to the level of cooks. Their password is *Nabuzardan,* supposedly in honor of Nebuchadnezzar's general or chef of chefs, clearly an allusion to Charlemagne's knights' victory cry "Montjoie."

Constantly Rabelais plays with the identity of the Chitterlings, or sausages; now we see them as fearless warriors, now as mere comestible food which Friar John sends to the kitchen. This juxtaposition of identities leads to a surrealistic view of the scene, and the sheer number of Chitterlings gives the battle epic proportions:

Pantagruel rose to look over the wood, whirled back suddenly, and told us that our fears were justified. To the left, he had sighted a force of fat Chitterlings in ambush. To the right, a half-league away, a vast body of mighty, giantlike Chitterlings were marching resolutely toward us along the side of a little hill; they were progressing in battle formation to the tune of bagpipes, sheep's bladders . . . merry fifes and drums, bugles and trumpets. From the seventy-eight standards he could count, Pantagruel judged them to be forty-two thousand strong (IV, 36).

In the Pantagruel and Werewolf episode Rabelais followed epic tradition; God sided with the giant, admonishing him with "Hoc fac et vinces." In the Chitterlings episode, divine intervention has a most grotesque appearance:

"Out of the north, suddenly flew a huge, great, fat, gray swine, with wings as long and wide as the arms of a windmill. His plumage was crimson as the phinicoptera or flamingo . . . His eyes were fiery and as carbuncles, his ears were green as leekgreen emeralds; his teeth yellow as topaz; his tongue very long and black as jet; his feet white, diaphanous and transparent as diamonds" (IV, 41).

A complete transformation of ancient and medieval epic takes place; Rabelais reduces parody *ad absurdum,* as if once and for all he wanted to dispose of a tired genre and a technique much overdone. The description of the pig symbolizes in a way the distinct new flavor of the *Fourth Book;* namely, an emphasis on cold plasticity which contrasts with the gigantic physical matter of the first two books. The fantastic creations of the *Fourth Book* are characterized by their unreal and artificial physical composition; each resembles a huge balloon dangling in space that has a vaguely human shape.

At each available opportunity, Rabelais fails to refrain from extensive verbal fantasy. As soon as the slightest opening appears, he fills it to overflowing with the fertile contents of whole families of words. In the case of the Chitterlings, the occasion arises in the enumeration of the cooks who enter the sow. Since they will act as butchers, their names are directly related to meat; in some instances, Rabelais plays with the words "bacon" and "lard," inventing a whole series of derivatives: "We must add to the list Stiffbacon, Astolard, Sweetlard, Brunchbacon, Scrapbacon, Bastelard, Guybacon, Smellbacon, Fairbacon, Freshlard, Bitterbacon, Lagbacon, Oglebacon, Weighbacon, Scanbacon, Watchlard" (IV, 40). Submerged under outlandish creatures, grotesque elements, and verbal fantasy, the parody of the ancient and medieval epics disappears in the distance; it forms a fragile background against which the vivid artistic creations stand out.

No epic voyage leaves out the storm at sea, an episode which shows the courage of the heroes and casts them against the stronger forces of Nature. By extension, the storm scene is often a means of testing a character's purpose in life. Rabelais does not fail to follow tradition, but he only goes through the motions of parodying the classical storm scene; instead he uses the scene as a receptacle for his vast knowledge of nautical terms. In this scene he brings Panurge to the fore in order to mock him.

In *Pantagruel*, Panurge had shown some fear, but in the *Fourth Book* he shows more than a suggestion. In giving such a distinct trait to Panurge, Rabelais must have had Folengo in mind for the latter does the same thing with Cingar. What matters, though, is that in the *Fourth Book* Rabelais returns to the Panurge of the first book in order to develop one of his earlier traits. In view of his development in the intervening *Third Book*, Panurge has regressed; he no longer concerns himself with lofty questions but appears as his old self. Considered as a whole, Panurge's character attains its apex in the *Third Book*.

The description of the mounting waves at the beginning of the storm scene has a pseudo-epic tone: "Suddenly the sea swelled, roared, rose mountain-high from the depths of an abyss. Huge waves lashed the sides of our vessels. The northwester rose with, in its train, a terrific hurricane. Black clouds gathered ominously; the gale drove furious gusts whistling through our shrouds. From the heavens above came terrific sheets of lightning, deafening peals of thunder, rain, then hail poured down upon us" (IV, 18).

A further allusion to the epic occurs as Panurge, wishing he were on terra firma, exclaims: "Thrice happy, four times happy, the humble cabbage planter! O cruel Fates, when you were spinning my destiny, you might have made a cabbage-grower of me."

During a storm at sea, Virgil's Aeneas cries out that three times and four times happy are those who were left defending Troy's walls instead of losing their lives uselessly on the ocean; Homer had used the same expression. What a discrepancy between the wishes of Panurge and Aeneas! Hence the parody, for the expression "Three times and four times happy" must have been part of common knowledge in the sixteenth century.[7]

As the storm worsens, Panurge invokes countless saints to save him from death; he even promises to build a chapel to the Virgin Mary if she should spare him. Of course, he conveniently forgets his vow as soon as the danger has passed. Folengo's Cingar behaves in the same manner.[8] Meanwhile, when the sea is about to overtake him, Panurge momentarily escapes by drowning himself in a flow of onomatopoeic words: "Ulbulbulbugh! Grrwh! Upchkvomtchbg! . . . O-o-o-o-o-o-h! I sink, I drown, I peugh. Where is heaven? I cannot see where earth is! Ugh! the only elements left us are fire and water . . . Ububbubgrshlouwhftrz! Would that by God's mighty will, I were now in the abbey close at Seuilly! . . ." (IV, 20). Panurge's physical idleness and verbal activity are contrasted to Friar John's physical activity as the latter helps to maintain the ship afloat, and to Pantagruel's energetic aid as well as to his reflective and meaningful prayers. These three characters offer a graduated spectrum of human behavior, but Pantagruel epitomizes the proper human conduct under such circumstances.

In the *Third Book,* Pantagruel assumed the role of a wise and venerable being, thus losing all his gigantic traits of the first books. Whereas Panurge regresses from the *Third Book* to the *Fourth Book,* Pantagruel's characterization is consistent. As far as Panurge is concerned, the *Third Book* is a freakish exception in his behavior pattern. It would be mere conjecture to judge to what extent Rabelais wanted us to be conscious of the development of his character or to what extent he simply forced Panurge to fit the contextual requirements of the book at hand. If, for example, Rabelais's imitation of Folengo's Cingar resulted in a discrepancy of Panurge's character, such a deviation must not have been of overriding importance.

Above all, the storm episode emerges as an original creation which owes its uniqueness and superiority to the massive movement generated with its various scenes. Contrary to many of its predecessors, the episode is not narrated, but acted out; it is composed of animated dialogues that convey the action. One may think that the juxtaposition of orders and counterorders, with Panurge's incessant crying, produces confusion, but Rabelais uses this means to express the movement of the action. He pours into the description his considerable nautical vocabulary, which is derived from Spanish and Italian as well as French, dialects.[9] These verbal edifices and their sonorous qualities contribute to the dynamic nature of the scene. The storm has rightly been called an artistic prodigy. It shows the poet in Rabelais:

> Luff, luff, luff the helm.
> Done, done! said the sailors.
> Keep her up . . . bring her round . . . so, ho, high! . . .
> hoist, haul!
> Golden words! Friar John commented.
> Hoist, hoist; haul, haul! A little elbow grease,
> your guts into it, lads, and we've done the trick!
> Luff, luff, Starboard . . . helm . . .
> The storm is almost spent; a little longer my
> hearties! Praise God, our devils are slinging
> their hooks.
> Out with your sails!
> Larboard! larboard!
> Let her go!
> Slack man, give her slack . . . right! right!
> Slack, luff! (IV, 22)

III *Toward Verbal Magic*

What has been said of the parody in the *Fourth Book* holds true for the satire as well; both are more subtle than in earlier books, and both are overshadowed by the characters or by the development of the narrative. As in the earlier works, the legal profession and religion form the targets of Rabelais's satire. In the *Fourth Book*, he obliquely criticizes the legal profession by a complete reversal of roles; the technique closely resembles the one used with Bridlegoose. The grotesque satire results from the depiction of a topsy-turvy world. For this purpose, Pantagruel visits the island of "Procuration," sentence-serving, inhabited by the "Chicanous," Catchpoles, and those who seek quarrels or bumbailiffs.

In a comic twist, Rabelais turns the tables; instead of presenting ferocious bailiffs, he introduces meek men who get beaten every time they go to someone's house to serve sentence; hence the name Catchpole. The episode offers Rabelais an excuse to tell the story of the Lord of Basché who invited Catchpoles to a wedding so that they would be beaten and thus provide entertainment for the guests.[10] In a development of the story-telling begun as an art form in the *Third Book*, Rabelais then narrates a tale within a tale. To illustrate the pleasure derived from cruelty, Basché tells the story of some pranksters (the late medieval poet Villon is among them) who so scare a monk's horse that, in running away wild, it dismembers its rider. Panurge, appearing true to form as the cruel prankster of *Pantagruel,* in turn, narrates the episode of the Chicanous.

The Catchpoles end up by losing their identity, first because they are engulfed by the irrelevant scenes in which they find themselves, and second because they become robots. Rabelais stresses the automatism in their actions; driven by their rapacity for the blows without which they cannot live, they constantly go back to Basché, or to others, for more beatings. Judge Bridlegoose in the *Third Book* had vestiges of human behavior; he only distorted and misinterpreted men's customs and laws, but the Catchpoles appear as puppets popping out of jumping-jack boxes. Originally Rabelais wanted to show the bailiff's pecuniary rapacity; their mechanical behavior, however, shows their similarity to many others who people the *Fourth Book*. They soon become mere toys. In a carnage scene that could well be a parody of the episode at the vineyard of Seuillé, Friar John, upon payment of a nominal fee, "swung his staff manfully, thwacking and cracking Redsnout so lustily on belly and back, on head and legs that, as he fell to earth, a battered pulp, I feared for the Catchpole's death. Then he gave him his twenty crowns. But the churl rose, happy as a king—or a pair of kings, for that matter. His disappointed colleagues addressed the flagellator: 'Master Devil-Friar, please take on some of us for less money'" (IV, 16).

The foremost episode dealing with religious satire is dominated by an outlandish eulogy, typical of the ones in the *Third Book*. The inhabitants of Papimania, land of pope worshiper, live in a society governed by Decretals, papal ordinances. Their greatest wish is to see the pope, as their first question indicates: "Have you seen him, good passengers, have you seen him?" (IV, 48). Without doubt, Rabelais intends to deride the concept of a human god on earth, or papal deification.[12] In a Lutheran vein he includes the whole facetious Chapter 53 praising the Decretals for their capacity to extract gold from France and direct it to Rome.

Henceforth Rabelais will endeavor, with avalanches of words, to ridicule both the Decretals and those who worship them. The stage for mockery is set when he names the leader of the Papimanes, Stoutmoron. This man's excessive praise of the Decretals casts a poor light on him and on the papal statutes because of the disproportion between his means and his purpose. Like Picrochole, Stoutmoron soon reaches a euphoric state and allows his warped imagination to overcome him:

O seraphic *Sextum!* How essential you are to the salvation of wretched humanity! . . . O cherubic *Clementinae!* How aptly you define and outline the functions of the perfect Christian! O angelic *Extravagantes!* How graciously you guard such wretched souls as wander in mortal shape through this vale of tears. Alas! when shall humanity receive, as a special gift of divine favor, the ability to abandon all other studies and pursuits? When shall men rise to that ecstatic state where they may read, learn, know, use, apply, practice, incorporate and sanctify you alone (IV, 51).

In order to show disrespect for the Decretals themselves, some of Pantagruel's companions encourage Stoutmoron to list the many vulgar uses to which they were put; among them, patterns for clothing, theatrical masks, and targets for arrows. Each time the result is disastrous, and while Rabelais smiles, the high priest cries out: "Divine vengeance!"

The reader might excuse Stoutmoron's ridiculous behavior if it were caused by innocence, but this character abhors what he calls heretics. However, Rabelais manages to steer away from vehement satire by causing Stoutmoron to vituperate against the heretics. The boundless quantity of his insulting epithets drowns out his anger:

Squeeze them between red-hot pincers, hold them over the flame, hack them to pieces, hang, draw and quarter them—it does no good. Pierce their breasts with spits, their conduits with rapiers; make mincemeat of them; fry, grill or broil them; split them in half; grind them to powder—it is labor lost. Pluck out their entrails; crush, pound, bash and smash them; snap their legs and arms off, roast them to ashes—you are no better off than when you started. These evil heretics remain decretalifuge (they run away from our *Decretals*), and decretalicide (they slay our canons!). Far worse, they are, then murderers, far worse then parricides. They are decretalictones (they assassainate the *Decretals*). They are very devils of hell! (IV, 53).

In this passage, typical of his art, Rabelais takes three words, break, burn, and murder, and expands upon them as if he were writing a variation on the theme of the meaning of these words, for the sheer pleasure of verbal manipulation. Consequently, the words take on a gratuitous role; meaning matters less than the playfulness involved in the cumulative process. As if this innumerable list did not suffice, Rabelais adds several neologisms whose learned qualities clash with their common counterparts.

The episode dealing with King Lent, the antithesis of the Chitterlings, best illustrates the tenuous link that exists between satire and fantasy. Superficially it seems that Rabelais wishes to show his disapproval of Lent, but this aim is incidental. King Lent is a gigantic plastic personification, composed of a lengthy enumeration of similes minutely describing his physical and moral attributes. Although each simile indirectly derides this creature, it subsists because of its intrinsic value and originality.

In King Lent's general portrait, Rabelais shows his subtle scorn for this character-institution by means of an ardent irony. Lent is associated with what he looks like. The features, customs, and laws of this fasting period are transposed to the physical characteristics of King Lent and contribute to the creation of a grotesque personage. In other words, the abstract and the moral are used concretely. This inversion of concrete and abstract further enhances the deforming process: "A huge greedy-guts, a glutton for peas, a crook fingered splitter of herring barrels, a mackerel-snatcher, an overgrown molecatcher, a great nestfeatherer. . . . He is a fernchinned demi-giant with a double tonsure to his crown . . . he is in the light business, and ready to sell candles on the slightest provocation. He is the standard bearer of the fish eater, the dictator of Mustardland, a flogger of small children and a calciner of ashes . . . he swarms with pardons, indulgences, stations . . ." (IV, 29).

Rabelais needs three chapters (Chapters 30–32), composed of similes, in which he gives free rein to his fantasy to describe King Lent's anatomy. The objects to which anatomical parts are compared have originality in the sense that a sharp contrast results from their juxtaposition. In such instances, the concrete appendage is described by an equally concrete object: "His toes suggest the keyboard of a spinet, his nails gimlets, his feet guitars, his heels clubs, his soles crucibles, his legs bird snares, his knees stools, his thighs cross-bowstrings-winders" (IV, 31).

A second group of similes transforms the abstract into concrete terms. This technique, which produces a more striking contrast than did the previous example, borders more often than not on the incongruous, although a faint bit of logic reinforces the image: "His memory reminds you of a scarf, his common sense of a great bell's chime, his imagination of a carillon. His thoughts suggest a flight of starlings; his conscience an unnestling of young herons; his deliberation a sack of barley, the grains rattling at the slightest shift . . ." (IV, 30).

In a study devoted to the description of King Lent's anatomy, one critic tries to show the validity of Rabelais's anatomical knowledge by distorting the object in the majority of cases to make it fit the physical part. When unsuccessful in his attempts, he criticizes Rabelais for his inaccuracy.[13] In each simile, of course, there is some resemblance between the compared parts, but Rabelais's imagination soon distorts reality. The reader ought to take into account the fact that Rabelais does not necessarily attempt to be plausible.

In the final analysis, this long catalogue of comparisons constitutes nothing other than an extraordinary exercise of the imagination; any attempt to make it plausible will meet with failure. We have here a swarm of similes; each one should be savored individually on its own merit, without regard for any logical sequence. One need not assimilate the whole; one can pick here and there allowing his own taste to dictate its liking. Indeed, the more irrational a comparison appears at first sight, the more effective it proves to be.

Rabelais reaches a climax in his experiments with wordplay in the episode of the Thawed Words. As Pantagruel and his companions travel in the North Pole region toward Master Gaster's domain, they are showered with frozen words that melt soon after they land on the ship. Rabelais could have found similar narratives in Plutarch or in the works of his Italian contemporaries: Castiglione's *Courtier* or Calcagnini's tales. One may also seek some ingenious meaning behind the fable of the Thawed Words that might fit in with Rabelais's evangelism or protestantism, but the episode remains a masterful and poetic verbal achievement—the ultimate in the fusion of image and meaning.[14]

In the fable of the Thawed Words, Rabelais gives a most complex value to words. He begins by playing with their form, making them concrete objects; in fact, they become merchandise which is readily handled. At the same time they are completely independent of their usual uses in that they bear no real relation to their meanings. Rabelais assigns them colors by using a metaphoric vocabulary drawn from heraldry: "They looked like sugarplums of various colors. Some were *gules* or red, others *sinople* or green, others *azure* or blue, others *sable* or black, others *or* or gold." (IV, 56). Having given the words color, he proceeds to endow them with sounds expressed by means of onomatopoeia: "There were horrible words and others, most unpleasant to behold; when they melted we heard: "Hink, hink, hink, hink, ticketty tock, briddety broddety, foo-froo-froo, bubbub boo, boobeddy-bood, boo-boo-boo-boo-boo; track-track, tracketty-track, trr, trr, trr, trrrrrrr! Haw-haw-haw-wheeeeee! gog-atty-gog, gog, gog, magog!" (IV, 56). In exhausting the words of all their poetic possibilities, forms, sounds, and colors, Rabelais seeks their symbolic values. Thus he creates a cosmic language which attains in an onomatopoeic jumble the expressive limits of words as if the task of the writer or the poet were to seize ghostly voices from the air and bring them to life in his hands.

The *Fourth Book* represents the ultimate blossoming of Rabelais's fantasy because of the number and quality of its episodes. Satire and parody form only the background of the work since they appear in merely a superficial manner; the episodes stand as independent creations into which Rabelais has profusely poured his verbal inventiveness, his playful imagery, his astute and animated story-telling, and his newer type of giganticism. The feats of the giants Gargantua and Pantagruel belong to another era; instead, the *Fourth Book* teems with clownish, puffed up, amorphous figures. Rabelais achieves surrealism with these strange shaped creatures, who claim human appearances or functions, and with his cumulative and almost gratuitous verbal display.

CHAPTER 5

From Self-Advertisement to Verve

SOME critics thought that the prologues to Rabelais's works tell in an overly elaborate fashion little that could not be said in a very few words.[1] In a sense, the same criticism would also hold true for Rabelais's works as a whole if one were to judge as these critics. Supposedly each prologue introduces the subject matter of the book that follows, as though it were a "commercial," but this purpose disappears in Rabelais's later work. Instead, the prologues become an outlet for experimentation with certain themes and techniques found in the respective books. The prologues warrant separate analysis because each one is a creative synthesis of the work it precedes, and together they demonstrate the essential artistic evolution of the author. A study of the prologues leads to a full understanding of the books as a whole.

I The Embryonic Prologue

In the prologue to *Pantagruel*, Rabelais does not deny his debt to the *Gargantuine Chronicles*. In fact, he states emphatically that he chose to narrate the giants' adventures because of the popularity of the subject matter. "Within two months the printers sold more copies of this work [*Chronicles*] than they will sell Bibles for nine years." He does not intend to immortalize Pantagruel, because oral tradition, by transmitting the tale from one generation to another, has already performed this task. Nor does he wish to hide his intention to parody medieval and Renaissance romances of chivalry for he mentions such "works of high timber . . . as *Fessepinte* or *Whip Pot, Orlando Furioso, Robert the Devil, Fierabras the Saracen Giant, William the Fearless, Huon of Bordeaux, Mandeville the Traveller,* and *Matabrune*. In a technique typical of burlesque, Rabelais includes two nonexistent titles, *Whip Pop* and *Matabrune,* among the real works, as if to mock the latter or to purposely confuse the reader with the two levels of titles.

Essentially the character of the first prologue is popular, Rabelais achieves this tone by addressing the reader directly in a rather flattering manner: "O most illustrious and most valorous champions, gentlemen and all others who delight in honest entertainment and wit." Most noteworthy is the fact that Rabelais uses somewhat broad appellations, whereas in subsequent books he addresses himself to a more specific audience, the drinkers. At this early date, wine has not yet become the symbol of truth, knowledge, or the joy of life. Rabelais is still in the formative stages of his creative progress.

The prologue's function consists primarily in praising the contents and insisting on its veracity. Both of these purposes lend themselves easily to the popular character of the prologue and the ensuing narrative. The end of the first prologue foreshadows the end of *Pantagruel;* it has the same playful quality as the last paragraph of the book proper because of its endless imprecations, whose exaggerated quantity causes the loss of serious meaning. Both the prologue and the ensuing book terminate on a whimsical and inconsequential note; from the beginning, Rabelais taunts the reader by leaving him with a jesting impression:

Before I conclude this prologue, I hereby deliver myself body and soul, belly and bowels, to a hundred thousand basketfuls of raving devils, if I lied so much as one throughout the work. By the same token, may Saint Anthony sear you with his erysipelatous fire . . . may Mahomet's disease whirl you in its epileptic jitters . . . may the festers, ulcers and chancres of every purulent pox infect, scathe, mangle and rend you, entering your bumgut as tenuously as mercurialized cow's hair . . . and may you vanish into an abyss of brimstone and fire, like Sodom and Gomorrah, if you do not believe implicitly what I am about to relate in the present *Chronicles* . . . (*P*, Prologue).

Another of Rabelais's preferred techniques appears here; he likes the details to accumulate. The more precisely he writes, the more ludicrous he renders the topic in question, because the lack of reality in the situation is demonstrated thereby.

In praising the contents of his first book, Rabelais attributes comforting and healing qualities to it by implication and by comparison. For example, he claims that the *Chronicles* put between two warm pieces of cloth and applied to the cheek can cure a toothache. One can easily discern the popular flavor in such a device. There is an oblique, but innocent, religious satire in his assertion that if the *Life of Saint Margaret* is read by women in labor to bring about good results then his *Pantagruel* can also have beneficial properties.

Each time Rabelais praises his work he uses a metaphor; eventually the image takes on an intrinsic esthetic value and an independent life that overshadows the insincere praise. Rabelais describes a hunting scene (p. 161) which results in a failure to track down the deer, or he depicts a falcon that lets its would-be prey escape; as a result, the hunters relate some episodes from the *Chronicles* and thus shrug off their disappointment. This metaphorical tableau my suggest to those who seek a more esoteric meaning that the spirit of *Pantagruel* can relieve the minds of men who are in search of the uncertain or unattainable. Here Rabelais may intend to imply that his books have an important value and function, but to what extent he jests remains an open question: "Is there not greater profit in them than a rabble of critics would have you believe?" This question and the above image already echo the famous metaphor in *Gargantua* of the dog extracting the bone marrow.

The second metaphorical tableau shows Rabelais's mastery of concrete imagery and the ascending role he gives it beyond mere comparison. It also stresses the therapeutic function of the work but does so almost incidentally because the series of similes it contains dominates the description: "What shall I say of those wretched devils plagued by pox and gout? How often they have appeared before us saturated with quicksilver ointment, salves and grease. Their faces shone like a larder keyhole . . . their teeth danced in their heads like the keyboards of an organ or spinet under the fingers of a maestro . . . they foamed at the gullet like a boar at bay in the toys of a pack of bloodhounds . . . What did they do in this crisis? Their sole consolation was to have somebody read them a few pages of this book." The comparisons form a sort of trajectory; they touch on hunting, then music, and finally come back to the hunting theme. Consequently, the metaphoric curve creates a movement because of the succession and the arrangement of its similes. Rabelais's unexpected juxtapositions also contribute to the striking and humorous quality of these comparisons.

Other stylistic techniques with which Rabelais is associated were added by him in later editions. Somewhat vulgar plays on words have replaced some irreverent religious remarks: "I speak like St. John in the Apocalypse: *'Quod vidimus testamur,* we relate what we have seen.' Or rather I quote his words like some lusty Thurifer (should I say Turdifer?) of the Martyr Lovers, or some terrifying Torrefier of the affections [allusions to a rather worldly group of theologians]."

The same kind of grotesque satire occurs where Rabelais uses another of his favorite stylistic devices, the accumulation of synonyms: "If anyone contradicts me, let him be herewith denounced as a false prophet, a champion of predestination, a poisoner and seducer of the people." In such multisynonymic constructions, Rabelais amplifies the common rhetorical or ciceronian technique of adding a synonym to stress a point and to give more eloquence to an idea. Rabelais always distorts; consequently he produces three or four synonyms, thus transforming the original mannerism into a playful and superfluous device that fits his own effervescent temperament. The author means to attack some clergy, but the pun and the vulgarity purposely veil the satire and cause it to lose its pungency. In rewriting various parts of his books, Rabelais added synonyms wherever possible. In the following case, Rabelais found three synonyms in the first edition of 1532: "false prophet," "poisoner," and "seducer of the people"; but he added to the definitive edition of 1542, "a champion of predestination" in order to be more specific and strike directly at the Calvinists while simultaneously enhancing the spoofing effect of the enumeration.

Considered as a whole, the prologue to *Pantagruel* adheres rather closely to the norms prescribed for such an introductory chapter; in an ironic context, it praises bluntly and defends vehemently the authenticity of the work. This defense occurs within a popular background which is evocative of hawking cries at fairs. Because the first prologue sticks to the point and stays within bounds it is the shortest of all. At the same time, owing to the self-imposed restrictions mentioned above, it is the least original. Of course, there are happy moments (although at times added later) such as the images, some precursory sense devices, and some oblique allusions to the kinds and subjects of satire and parody. In the final analysis, the merits of the prologue to *Pantagruel* are those of an embryonic Rabelais who is still groping to find his right medium; the first book supports such an assertion.

II *The Prologue as an Exercise in Imagery*

In the prologue to *Gargantua*, Rabelais matures into a creative artist. Although he praises what will follow, he abandons the more popular and simple device of attempting to convince the reader of the authenticity of the book and thereby jesting with his credulity. Instead Rabelais chooses another method of playing with us: he discusses the meaning of *Gargantua*. This prologue reflects a high level of sophistication; it does not pretend to address the ordinary reader, nor does it have the market-place boasting tone of *Pantagruel*. It contains erudite allusions to antiquity which contrast with the rather plebeian tone of the first prologue. Only the beginning phrases and the ending sentences bear any relation to the therapeutic and protesting quality pervading the first prologue: "Hail, O most valiant and illustrious drinkers! Your health, my precious pox ridden comrades! To you alone I dedicate my writings." The first allusion to drinkers ought to be noted only because it announces one of the prevailing themes in the remaining works but also because it foreshadows and sets the stage for one of the most crucial arguments of the prologue. Compared to the first prologue, the end to this prologue is much more subdued and much less gratuitous. Rabelais merely abides by the form ordinarily prescribed for such occasions. A lonely imprecation appears as if it were an afterthought: "And you, donkey-pizzles, hark!—may a canker rot you! . . ."

The prologue to *Gargantua* consists of a composite of juxtaposed images whose variations convey a supposedly contrasting meaning. To support his thesis in the prologue, that the book may have a frivolous appearance but a very deep philosophical significance, Rabelais adopts the method of antithesis as his key stylistic device. He offers initially an interplay of two images in his description of the *sileni*, small apothecary boxes whose exterior bore grotesque figures but whose interior contained a number of rare drugs. To prove his point, he uses Socrates as an example, indicating that the philosopher's physical ugliness hid a most brilliant mind; at this time, however, he wilfully confuses the image of the *sileni* with that of the Greek.

In this prologue, Rabelais proceeds by means of parallel stylistic constructions, as well as contrasting parallelisms. In describing the *sileni*, first he gives the exterior objects: "fantastically painted figures of harpies, satyrs, bridled geese, hares with gigantic horns, saddled ducks, winged goats in flight, harts in harness and many other droll fancies." He then counters with a description of the interior: "priceless drugs such as balsam of Mecca, ambergris from the sperm whale, amomum from the cardamon, musk from the deer and civet from the civet's arsehole—not to mention various sorts of precious stones, used for medical purposes, and other invaluable possessions." In typical fashion, the bulk of the enumeration is vulgar while the remnant is incidental; this contrast between the sublime, or the erudite, and the vulgar condenses the very spirit of the book. The same contrasting symmetrical construction occurs in a portrait of Socrates which may also be a prototype of Rabelais himself:

Alcibiades [one of the philosopher's students] likened Socrates to these boxes, because judging by his exterior, you would not have given an onion skin for him. He was ill-shaped, ridiculous in carriage, with a nose like a knife, the gaze of a bull and the face of a fool. His ways stamped him a simpleton, his clothes a bumkin. Poor in fortune, unlucky when it came to women, hopelessly unfit for all office in the republic, forever laughing, forever drinking neck to neck with his friends, forever hiding his divine knowledge under a mask of mockery. . . . Yet had you opened this box you would have found in it all sorts of priceless, celestial drugs: immortal understanding, wondrous virtue, indomitable courage, unparalleled sobriety, unfailing serenity . . . (*G*, Prologue).

In the handling of these metaphors, we see Rabelais's affinity for expansion, now on a lofty plane. He develops his metaphors when there is no rational need to do so except the simple pleasure of creativity. But the prologue has some rough-hewn edges in its transitions. Suddenly, either in keeping with the theme set in the opening sentence or in an attempt to insert a popular note, he asks: "Have you ever uncorked a bottle of wine? God help us, do you remember the look on your face?" This irrelevant question introduces the next image, the most famous one in the prologue, if not in all the books: "Or have you ever seen a dog fall on a marrow bone?" To build up suspense and tension, Rabelais produces five clauses beginning with "how" and three with "what" describing the dog's conflict with the bone; the crescendo collapses on a purposely ironic "Nothing but a little marrow." To make the idea of seeming and being more effective, the moral continues the canine imagery. Rabelais takes great pleasure in toying with this metaphor: "Modelling yourself upon the dog, you should be wise to scent, to feel and to prize these fine, full-flavored volumes. You should be fleet in your pursuit of them, resolute in your attack."

Irony marks much of the prologue. Rabelais expresses one thing but often means the opposite. Overstatement and understatement are additional forms of contrast. Having just finished saying that the reader ought to look for some abstruse meaning in his work, Rabelais does a sudden about-face and declares that his book is of little value, for "in composing this masterpiece, I have not spent or wasted more leisure than is required for my bodily refection." Pursuing his argument about the significance and value of *Gargantua,* he introduces the idea that a literary work may smell of wine or oil, metaphors for a light-headed composition or a profound and carefully created book. He asserts sardonically that he prefers to glory in wine rather than oil. To express this conviction, he adopts a stylistic device that is part of his trademark; he piles up several adjectives, or adverbs, with identical-sounding suffixes and thus produces a movement, which conveys his enthusiasm for the subject at hand: "How much more reconciling, smiling and beguiling wine is than oil!"

Because of the wilful ambiguity of the prologue to *Gargantua,* some critics have drawn the oil from Rabelais's works; others, the wine. Some find it necessary to extract a philosophical marrow, others prefer to interpret the marrow as an artistic and creative sense. Taking Homer as an example, Rabelais warns those who would draw the oil: "Do you honestly believe that Homer, penning his *Iliad* or *Odyssey* never dreamed of the allegorical patchwork subsequently inflicted upon him by Plutarch, by Heraclides Ponticus, by Eustathius, by Cornutus the Stoic or by Politian, the Italian who filched his criticism from the lot of them?"

In interpreting an author's thought one should ascertain what he intended in his work and not merely read something into it that is foreign to his ideas. Of course, the line between the two can be hard to discern. One must also distinguish between what the author meant at the time of its creation and what the work means today. On the other hand, esthetically speaking, the critic can read something into a work that the author did not consciously intend without diminishing the validity of this criticism; on the contrary, such evaluations enhance the value of the work and unveil the writer's intuitive creativity. Chapter 7 will deal with Rabelais's thought. Seen in an esthetic light, however, the prologue to *Gargantua* can be considered an exercise in imagery. In the prologue to *Pantagruel*, Rabelais uses unnecessary and plain words that repeat an argument to advertise his work; but in the second book, although the prologue still serves basically as an advertisement, he moves up to a higher esthetic level by presenting several extended images to convey a single idea.

III *Toward Subjectivity and Self-Defense*

The prologue to the *Third Book* contrasts strikingly with the two earlier prologues. Gone are the boasting claims that were already on the wane in *Gargantua*. In the twelve years between the second and the third books, Rabelais's skill in writing prologues improved. This prologue has lost the greater part of the popular character found in the earlier works. It is instead a very personal exposition of the author's feelings at the time of the composition of the book. Among other innovations one distinguishes the use of digressions and tales, a flowery style that smacks of Ciceronianisms and Humanism, the increasing dominance of erudition and allusions to the ancients already apparent in *Gargantua,* and finally propaganda for François I's war effort against Charles V.[2] Stylistically speaking the prologue truly represents an antechamber to the *Third Book*.

Structurally, the prologue is divided into two parts. Using a technique which goes back to *Gargantua*, Rabelais first introduces the image of Diogenes, the Greek philosopher, who, instead of helping to build the defenses of Corinth, went to a nearby hill and rolled up and down in his barrel as a gesture of complete contempt. Rabelais, of course, compares himself to

Diogenes and declares that instead of helping to defend France against the invader, he will roll his own barrel, by writing the *Third Book*. At least he can console himself about his physical inactivity because his barrel contains some of that divine wine to which he had given great meaning in *Gargantua*.

The image of Diogenes and the Corinthian defenders is the highlight of the prologue and one of the most successful endeavors in all of Rabelais's books. In developing it Rabelais broke down all restraining barriers; this represents the author at his best in the midst of dynamic verbal creation. When we remember that he took the incident from Lucian, who simply states that the Greek philosopher "rolled with great zeal the barrel which he used as a lodging, ascending and descending the Craneum," [3] we realize the astonishing and overwhelmingly expansive achievement which the author produced in this metaphor:

. . . amid a great straining of arms, he wheeled and whirled it about, shoving it here, pushing it there . . . pulling it one way, tugging it the other . . . tumbling it one side up, then overturning it again . . . whifting, thrusting, driving, jostling and hustling it every which way . . . now impelling it to the left, now hurtling it to the right, jogging it here, butting it there . . . beating, slamming, dashing, banging and kicking it . . . sending it crashing downhill from the heights of Craneum into the valley, then rolling it up again, like a new Sisyphus with his legendary stone . . . (III, Prologue).

Rabelais lists hundreds of arms to describe the activities of the Corinthians. He creates movement in the prose of the above passage simply by using verbs. In some instances he varies the movement with a series of verbs and direct objects: "others fortified the walls of the city, raised bastions, squared outworks, dug trenches . . ."; in others, he affixes many objects to a single verb, thus switching from a regular rhythmic pace to a more prolonged and choppy one: "Some worked on bows, slings, crossbows, pellets, catapults, grenades, firebrands, scorpions, ballistas and other engines . . ."

The image of Diogenes is not a fortuitous one for the outcome of the *Third Book*. Since the Greek's philosophy abounds with cynicism and doubt, it casts a revealing light on what follows. Through this metaphor, Rabelais announces the spirit in which Panurge operates; defeat looms before the struggle has begun.

Hence Diogenes becomes the very symbol of the *Third Book*. The myth of Sisyphus, which is alluded to by Rabelais, further enhances for the modern reader the feeling of absurdity which trails the quest for happiness.

In the prologue to the *Third Book*, to a great extent Rabelais employs digressions, the longest of which is the image of Diogenes that assumes such huge proportions. Within this monumental digression, Rabelais, addressing the reader, takes off on more tangents: "Certainly you must possess an undefinable something [Trojan ancestry] that was his [Diogenes]. A quality indeed, which the ancient Persians prized most highly in their spies . . . a faculty the Emperor Antonius Caracalla specially exacted of his confidential servants . . . a gift which gave the Rohan serpentine its surname [allusion not known]. . . ."

The most striking digression which appears in the second part of the prologue is a somewhat lengthy narration which recounts Ptolemy's attempts to win the love of the Egyptians by offering them a two-humped black camel of rare species from Asia and a "curiously complexioned slave, half black, half white, not horizontally divided in colors (like the female votary of Venus seen by Appollonius of Tyana) but vertically." The Egyptians react negatively and reject these gifts because they prefer the harmonious to the grotesque. Usually Rabelais uses a narrative of this nature to prove a moral or fact which has already been stated; this one dangles until he explains that in the past he thought he was satisfying a large public with his first two books but that he only aroused the wrath of the theologians from the Sorbonne.

As already noted, Rabelais makes a different and more frequent use of short stories in the *Third Book* than in his previous works; the prologue anticipates this prominent device of the book that follows. The digressions form an integral part of the new narrative technique. Although the shortest distance between two points is a euclidean straight line, the "scenic route" holds many artistic attractions. At first sight, digressions may seem to create hopeless confusion, but an enriched and vital orderliness can be brought out of apparent chaos as Montaigne, the master of this technique, was to prove some forty years later. Through digressions an author arrives at a prismatic view of his subject matter very much in the cubist vein by superimposing various related facets of the discussion.

The digressions in the third prologue are one of the chief outlets for Rabelais's classical learning; each divergent narrative is drawn from antiquity. The prologue has a much more learned character than the two earlier ones, and this new tone carries over into the *Third Book,* replacing the popular tone of the first two prologues and books. Rabelais no longer must prostitute himself in order to sell his books; he can now display his humanism without dipping into the lower reaches of plebeian literature. Of course, there are still some vulgar or obscene allusions, but a generally high level of eloquence characterizes the prologue. This lofty tone results partially from long and involved sentences in imitation of ciceronian rhetoric; in such instances, Rabelais shares a trait, if not a mania, of other humanists, which often results in inextricable meanings.

Rabelais cannot refrain from juggling with rhetorical devices —be it the antithesis: "Did not Ennius, drinking, write and writing drank? Did not Aeschylus (if Plutarch's *Symposiacs* deserve credence) quaff while composing and quaffing compose?"—or the Ciceronian repetition: "Then they imbibe freely, frankly, resolutely." Neither can he, nor does he want to, avoid the juxtaposition of the learned and the common; in toying with words, he seeks out alliterations and assonances: "au son de ma musette mesureray la musarderie des musars" ("I shall play my bagpipe till the mellowtones raise yellow stones"); "Feust-ce portant botte, cachant crotte, ployant rotte ou cassant motte . . ." ("I would gladly have lugged hods, shelled pods, dug sods or broken clods"). After a long, elegant ciceronian sentence in which he tries to defend his lack of participation in the feverish war activity, Rabelais returns to a low key, thus producing the usual contrast between the sublime and the vulgar, here by means of very common but concrete similes. "Tell me what honor falls to such a merely look on, liberal with their eyes but niggardly with their efforts . . . hoarding their money . . . scratching their scalps like louts and oaves . . . gasping at flies like tithe calves . . . wagging their ears like Arcadian asses at the melody of the musicians, and with expressionless mien, approving of the performance. . . ."

From Self-Advertisement to Verve

Rabelais signs his real name to the *Third Book* and claims authorship for the first time. The reason for this is his official permission from King François I to publish the book. As a result of the grant, he deems it tactful to show his appreciation by defending the king's policy against Charles V. The Diogenes image represents the French war effort in 1546 in one of its senses, and Rabelais's excuse to the king for writing instead of fighting follows it. Soon, however, the real reason for Rabelais's propaganda in favor of the king becomes apparent. Almost unrecognized by the reader, the warriors and defenders of Corinth, that is, Paris, assume a completely different identity; they suddenly loom as theologians from the Sorbonne. François I may have had his hands full with Charles V, but Rabelais, too, far from being idle, has been waging a war against these theologians who, in his opinion, have maligned him.

In 1542, Rabelais had revised the first two books trying unsuccessfully to make them palatable to these gentlemen. Now behind the shield of the king's protection he can at last lash out against the sophists and proclaim his woes publicly. He accuses them of misinterpreting his work, thus keeping it from being appreciated by his contemporaries. Therefore he feels no guilt in attacking them boldly and vehemently, finally calling them wretched dogs: "As for holier than thou hypocrites, I would suffer them still less gladly, even though they be finished tosspots, hardshell crusties of the pox, afflicted with an unquenchable thirst and an inexhaustible hunger. . . . Back, curs, to hell! Out of my way, back from the barrel, out of the sunlight, you scum of the devil. To your flock, mastiffs, fly hence, buzzards . . . Grrrrrr, Grrrrr! Kssssss! Ksssss!" Although grotesque images and onomatopoeia alleviate the attack, the prologue ends on an angry —and in the last sentences obscene—note. This vulgarity may placate Rabelais himself but it gives the ending an abruptness typical of the preceding prologues, especially the one to *Pantagruel.*

However, the basic differences between the introductions to the first and third books is that the former has a certain gratuitousness in its satirical attack on the monks and theologians, whereas in the latter Rabelais expresses a feeling very close to his heart. In the third prologue, Rabelais departs drastically from previously established patterns. The change from an objective to a subjective approach allows this prologue to be regarded as a lament, and at times a protest, in which the author complains about the established order's mistreatment. Yet the thesis of the prologue transcends this complaint and the attack on the destructive theologians. It takes the form of a bitter and defiant conviction, recalling the second prologue, that his contemporary critics do not extract the proper "marrow"; here the bone becomes the barrel "lively at the source of perpetual flow, a veritable cornucopia of merriment and mockery." Rabelais protests that essentials other than the religious content of his works—whatever that might be—ought to be judged. Doesn't this outcry prove that the imaginative vein takes precedence over a system of ideas? Of course, if one sees irony throughout the opposite view becomes valid. But how can one ascertain definitely when Rabelais means what he says and when he does not? One thing is certain: a shift from mere advertisement to defense of what follows appears in the prologues.

IV *Autobiography Superseded by Digression*

The prologue to the *Fourth Book* is the culmination of that literary form because in it Rabelais has completely appropriated the form and made it his own; the three earlier prologues, like three streams, converge to produce one broad river. Rabelais no longer needs to boast about the quality or value of his work or to defend its purpose; he can abandon himself to his imagination as it shifts from one story to another. His affinity for digression causes it to become an important device in the *Fourth Book*. His penchant for story-telling and his increased interest in erudition and antiquity have blossomed fully. The subjectivity noticed in the third prologue reaches a quasi-autobiographical level.

As the reader eventually finds out, the central theme of the fourth prologue is supposed to be health. Rabelais discusses the subject rather briefly at the beginning and comes back to it again at the end where he concludes that good health is more important than economic well-being. One cannot help but detect an autobiographical strain in this preoccupation. In 1552, date of the publication of the *Fourth Book*, Rabelais was about sixty and at most, a year away from his death. No doubt he must have been in failing health at that time. Furthermore, to substantiate his argument in the prologue, he introduces another personal element. Quoting two famous Greek physicians and the Bible, he discusses doctors who spend their lives curing others but are themselves decrepit. Does not Rabelais, a doctor himself, identify his own life with these? He concludes, finally, that anyone who lacks good health ought to pray that God grant it to him.

The word "prayer," begins a chain reaction that not only becomes the artificial foundation for the development of the ensuing tales but also the tenuous link which connects them. Whereas the first digression in this category—God's answer to Zacchaeus' prayers to see Christ—proves the point of praying, the second one, which deals with the son of a prophet who loses his ax in the water and has it retrieved by God's wish, serves as a transition to the main fable in the prologue concerning Couillatris, Puddingballocks, who loses his ax and prays to Jupiter for its restitution.[4] This last tale, derived from Aesop but considerably expanded by Rabelais, is interrupted several times, by other irrelevant stories. As a result, Puddingballocks shares the spotlight with Jupiter who is seen holding court on Mount Olympus and listening to Priapus' tales. Rabelais succeeds in bringing the Olympic scene to life by shuffling the time concept, that is, by transposing Jupiter's actions into his own times and then shifting the events back into antiquity. The king of the gods describes his decisions involving Ivan the Terrible and the Tartars, the shereef of Morocco, Prince Maurice of Saxony, Henry II of France and discusses the merits of three leading theologians, Peter Ramus, Peter Galland, and Peter de Cognière. He mentions the last three only, it would seem, to play with their given name, Pierre (stone).

The fourth prologue exteriorizes Rabelais' dynamic and overflowing imagination more than any other. Many scenes have no logical *raison d'être* for appearing in his work; they acquire validity and identity by the very fact that they are included. A case in point occurs in one of Priapus' dissertations. Playing upon the obscenities associated with his name, this character suddenly names some sixty European musicians, whom he has heard singing dubious ballads.[5] Why such a cascade of names? Although this enumeration allows Rabelais to exhibit yet another area of his encyclopedic knowledge, it is valuable above all because it exhibits his superabundant fantasy.

After repeatedly juggling with the word "cognée," ax, and its suggested obscene meaning, Rabelais settles on an anticlimactic moral for his lengthy tale. Having been offered a golden, silver, or ordinary ax, Puddingballocks chooses the one that originally belonged to him; for this noble action, Mercury, Jupiter's emissary, gives him the other two as well. As in Voltaire's *Candide*, Rabelais advises to "seek, rather moderation, and you shall have your wish, and the better, too, if you work hard meanwhile." The didacticism, however, is strongly overshadowed by the towering narrative. As in the case of La Fontaine's fables, the reader is not attracted to the worn out though universal moral at the end but to the artistic and poetic qualities of the tale.

In the prologue to the *Fourth Book*, Rabelais reaches a sophisticated level of narration through his digressions and their outgrowth, the story within a story. There is one more instance of a tale within a tale in that work: "How an Old Woman of Popefiggery Fooled the Devil" (IV, 47). The increased use of digressions in the prologue bears a close relationship to the surrealistic creatures in the book which follows, in that the former foreshadows the new type of grotesque found in the latter. Each new digression further distorts the essential thesis acting as an appendage to the central narrative. Thus the Puddingballocks episode with its various digressions and stories within stories appears to be a huge growth tacked on to the health theme; as a whole it resembles any one of the monstrous deformed creations which people the *Fourth Book*.

The prologue's center of gravity, the Jupiter scene with Priapus, has no connection with the avowed thesis, and its prominence throws the whole prologue off balance. The composite nature of the fourth prologue conveys the surrealism which pervades the whole book. However, one ought not to be deceived by its apparent chaos. Like Montaigne in his essays, Rabelais in the prologue first states the theme, then illustrates it profusely with examples, apparently irrelevant, and then finally returns to the original theme having enlightened it through the divergent offshoots.

Repetition is the basis of Rabelais's art, and the fourth prologue demonstrates the various uses of this ciceronian device which the author has successfully rejuvenated. The redundant repetition of the adverb *tant* ("so much") has an ironic purpose in the following quotation: "N'est-il pas escript et practiqué par les anciennes coustumes de ce tant noble, tant antique, tant beau, tant florissant, tant riche royaulme de France que le *mort saisit le vif?*" ["Consult the hallowed customs of the noble ancient, beauteous, wealthy and flourishing realm of France! Do they not warrant, in writing, that the dead seize the quick?"]

Another way Rabelais uses repetition consists in grouping together several synonymous verbs. This procedure inevitably leads to movement. Rabelais excels in the creation of movement, produced, in one way or another by heaping words on top of each other. He is a writer of action, the action of words as well as the action of characters: "Il trépigne, il trotigne, il s'efforce, il s'escarte, il monte sur un sycomore" ["He wriggled about, stood on tiptoe, trotted this way and that all in vain. At last he moved away and climbed a sycamore"]; "En cetuy estrif (embarrass) commença carier, prier, implorer, invocquer Juppiter" ["Lost in grief, Puddingballocks began to invoke Jupiter. He cried, begged, pleaded"]; "And they shouted and they prayed, and they lamented, and they invoked Jupiter with cries . . ."; "they specify who shall be cheated, swindled, bilked and diddled by their craft."

Movement also results from enumerating details, another form of verbal superfluity: "causing health to flee above or below, before or behind, to right or to left, within or without." At first sight, the details seem utterly confused, but upon a closer look, one notices that the author has followed an orderly pattern: "with the money he purchased a great many farms, barns, cottages, lodges, outhouses, meadows, vineyards, woods, plowlands, pastures, ponds, mills, gardens, willow groves, oxen, cows, ewes, sheep, goats, sows, porkers, asses, horses, roosters, capons, hens, pullets, geese, ganders, ducks, drakes and other things." The first part amplifies the word "farm." Beginning with "meadows," we have the description of the farm. Rabelais often groups contrasting words: cultivated and noncultivated lands, meadows-vineyards, woods-plowlands, gardens and willow groves, and ponds and mills. The third part enumerates farm animals either by opposite sexes, geese-ganders, or by association, asses-horses, roosters-capons. Hence the apparent "confusion" is movement composed of an organized accumulation of details.

An additional rhetorical trope, the antithesis, is another means of obtaining movement. The contrasting meanings produce a movement enhanced by Rabelais's use of the echo technique— the repetition of a word or its derivative. The movement results from the repetition of the same sounds; the words are repeated with different connotations: "without health is life life, is not life livable. . . . Without health life spells but languor; life spells but the appearance of death. Accordingly, if you aching (that is dead) seize the lively, seize life (that is health)." This passage may have a deeper significance in that it is typical of the antithetical interplay between life and death so cherished by baroque writers who inherited it from the Middle Ages. It is noteworthy that this baroque trait occurs in the prologue to a book which has been said to contain much "flamboyant gothic" [6] another baroque element that we have called surrealism. Hence, the fourth prologue foreshadows the ensuing book in more ways than one.

Popular elements based on the *Chronicles* disappear from the fourth prologue, with a few notable exceptions included in a parenthetical statement: "A few drops of divine [Jupiter's] sweat, falling on earth, produced what men call Cauliflower." However, the imagery of the prologue is characterized by the earthiness which pervades Rabelais's works. For example, the similes describing Jupiter and his court are derived from the vulgar and contrast with our idea of this ordinarily distinguished personage. The comparisons deprecate the gods by their very commonness: "Hereupon the venerable gods and goddesses burst into fits of laughter, whirling like a microcosm of flies"; "Jupiter twisted his head like a monkey swallowing a pill and assumed so awesome an expression that all Olympus trembled." Quite a discrepancy exists between a fly, a monkey, and the king of the gods. With the image of the flies, Rabelais has succeeded in making us visualize the movement of a person or a group laughing. The monkey simile is so much out of context that it completely vulgarizes the tableau.

In describing Puddingballocks as he receives his hatchet, Rabelais expresses the euphoric state of his character by means of another simile which contains an abrupt transposition: "Transported with joy, like a fox who meets a band of runaway hens, he grinned from ear to ear." Although the comparison brings to life a concrete and salient picture to express a state of mind, at the same time it unveils an incongruity. The woodsman does not have the cunning traits of a fox; on the contrary, he appears as a simple and honest individual. In order to realize its full potential, Rabelais allows the simile to stand on its own as an imaginative creation because it detaches itself from the context.

Since Rabelais prefers the ellipse to the straight line as his work progresses, he indulges himself more and more in lengthier prologues that are the prototypes of the books they precede. The prologues allow Rabelais to expound beyond thematic restrictions. They show Rabelais's assurance in the craft of narration that graduates into an expansive and rambling imagination. Each prologue contains a microcosm of its own. As the prologues lose their original boastful purpose, they grow closer esthetically to the respective books. The progession of the prologues follows the same line as the books: from imitation and restriction to boundless fantasy. Each prologue is an experimental endeavor which passes its test most successfully when it supersedes its introductory role and becomes nectar itself.

CHAPTER 6

Pedagogy Systematized and Surpassed

WITH the new and enlightened emphasis on learning in Rabelais's time, it is no wonder that the whole system of education came under close scrutiny, although with some notable exceptions, the results of this reassessment did not see the light until later. Rabelais joined the other humanists and created his own pedagogical formula for his two giants. Seen in retrospect, this system of education does not contain much originality, nor is it necessarily unique in relation to others elaborated at the time, but it deserves special study because it elaborates certain goals, transcending the centuries, toward which educators continue to strive.[1] In addition, it unveils another facet of Rabelais, his serious side. There can be no doubt that he is serious since he states his ideas forthrightly without couching them in comic or ironic terms.

To this didactic end, he adopts an eloquent rhetorical style; as a matter of fact, whenever he uses this tone in his writing, often in an oratorical or epistolary form, the particular passage has an educative or moral purpose. For Rabelais, as for any educator, pedagogy, religion, and morals form an integral part of education. His approach to learning gives a composite picture of the man and the writer; it contains some remnants of the Middle Ages, but the Renaissance dominates. His humanism (meaning his admiration for the ancients) appears in the ciceronian oratorical style that he predominantly adopts, although his exuberance cannot long remain in the background, and he often drowns the flowery prose in an outpouring of words. A study of Rabelais the educator shows us Rabelais the moralist, the thinker, the humanist, and the stylist; the particular becomes a basis for the whole.

I *Rabelais's Humanism*

In *Pantagruel*, the principal source of pedagogical discussion is Gargantua's letter to his son who has arrived in Paris to attend the university.[2] In a very elegant but sometimes tortuous style, the father advises him on what he should avail himself of in order to profit fully from his stay in the city of learning. The missive deals with education in abstract and theoretical terms; the practical aspects are discussed in *Gargantua*. Significantly the evolution in the creative process from the first to the second book holds true for the treatment of education; the development of this subject matter takes place in *Gargantua* after being tried out, so to speak, in *Pantagruel*. Generally, Gargantua's letter to Pantagruel is considered a key document for an assessment of Rabelais's religious thought, which will be analyzed in the next chapter, and his views on education, but it transcends these two interests in presenting the father's feelings for his son. This father wishes the best for his son who believes that the future holds brighter prospects for his son than the past in which he was brought up. In sum, the letter reflects the author's conviction in progress and in the advancement of civilization.

Gargantua speaks out against the Middle Ages with the typically prejudiced view of a Renaissance man: "We were still in the dark ages; we still walked in the shadow of the dark clouds of ignorance; we suffered the calamitous consequences of the destruction of good literature by the Goths" (*P*, 8). Gargantua's attitude resembles that of the Romantics who opposed the dark Middle Ages to the bright and learned Renaissance. Although Rabelais's position might be excused because of his nearness to the preceding era, the early nineteenth-century writers, who invented the term Renaissance, could have taken better advantage of the perspective of time. At any rate, the "suddenly there was light" opinion, expounded by Rabelais and others, has rightfully been changed. Today we view the Middle Ages as the beginning of a movement which culminates in the sixteenth century:[3] "Today, the old sciences are revived, knowledge is systematized, disciplines reestablished. . . . Today, the world is full of learned men, brilliant teachers and vast libraries" (*P*, 8).

Gargantua is advised to acquire a knowledge of all disciplines;

liberal arts, sciences, mathematics, law, medicine, religion, and military science. Critics have often reproached Rabelais for exacting too much from his student, even if he is a giant; at this point, however, the author is completely oblivious of verisimilitude. He no longer addresses a student, a giant, or any particular human being, but his times. He simply admonishes his contemporaries to accept, to drink in, all the knowledge now made available in a purified form and to discard the distorted and degenerate medieval learning. In his blind faith in the new era, he refuses to yield any credit, though deserved, to the Middle Ages.

Like other humanists, Rabelais admires the literature of antiquity for both its content and its style. As for the latter, he counsels: "Model your Greek style on Plato, your Latin on Cicero" (P, 8); by inference, he means that Plato should be followed for a poetic flowing prose, whereas Cicero offers a model of formality and eloquence. Rabelais also lists a few of the authors whom he reads for thought and historicity: "Now I delight in reading Plutarch's *Morals*, Plato's noble *Dialogues*, the *Monuments* of Pausanias and the *Antiquities* of Athenaeus" (P, 8.) These authors were not suddenly brought out of oblivion and read again. Medieval scholars knew the literature of antiquity well, but they used it primarily to substantiate Church dogma. The Renaissance humanists began to appreciate these texts for their intrinsic values, both philosophical and esthetic. They placed the works in their time of composition, all without taking the corrupting medieval commentaries into account, derived some universal truths from the classics, for they were not afraid to discover secular or non-religious knowledge. This re-evaluation constituted the rediscovery of antiquity.

As a result of this new scholarship, the Bible received the same treatment as other texts; it was to be read in the original version, without benefit of biased commentary: "Devote a few hours a day to the study of the Holywrit. Take up the New Testament and the Epistles in Greek; then, the Old Testament in Hebrew" (P, 8). Humanists wanted to know what the Bible said and not what had been said about it, even at the risk of interpreting it differently than the Church, which was usually the case. To this end, Gargantua encourages Pantagruel to learn Greek, Hebrew,

Chaldean, Arabic, and Latin so that he might be able to consult the Scriptures and the Koran in their earliest versions.

One aspect of Pantagruel's education deviates slightly from the intellectual path outlined earlier and contains some medieval overtones: "You are growing to manhood now; soon you will have to give up your studious repose to lead a life of action; you will have to learn to bear arms, to achieve knighthood, so as to defend my house and help our allies, frustrate the attacks of the evildoers" (*P*, 8). The knowledge of bearing arms is not by itself medieval—sons of noblemen received such instruction far into the nineteenth century—but the concept is couched in terms that clash with the over-all progressive tone of the letter: "to achieve knighthood"; the word "knighthood" rings false to the enlightened ear. Once again, a theoretical statement foreshadows an episode in the following book; this one is developed in *Gargantua* when the giant comes to rescue his father, Grandgousier, from Picrochole's "evildoers."

The description of the library of Saint Victor in *Pantagruel* gives an oblique view into Rabelais's concept of education; the approach is satirical rather than expository. The author criticizes the worthless books that crowd the libraries by producing an innumerable list of volumes bearing vulgar titles. On a larger scale, he seeks to ridicule medieval or scholastic education. Although he never explicitly states this aim, his purpose becomes apparent not only from the satirical catalogue but also from Gargantua's letter to Pantagruel which contrasts the old with the new era. Rabelais's first exposition of his ideas on education has a counterpart in *Gargantua* where he shows at length the giant's education under the scholastic method and then under modern tutors. The whole matter of Gargantua's tutorial and benevolent relationship with his son recurs at the beginning of the *Fourth Book*. At this point Pantagruel, about to set out in search of the Divine Bottle, receives a messenger who bears a letter wishing him Godspeed on his forthcoming voyage. At the end of the letter, the father writes his son: "I have come upon some diverting books, which the bearer will deliver to you. You may read them when you seek relaxation from your more serious studies" (IV, 3). Many years later, Gargantua continues to show interest in his son's education. The first letter to Pantagruel fits into a pattern from which we learn that Rabelais favors careful parental supervision of the education of children as well as parental pride.

Although Gargantua's education translates into action that which the letter to Pantagruel expresses abstractly, Rabelais further enlarges the theoretical scope of his views on education in the second book, namely the episode of the Abbey of Thélème. For example, he expands the number of foreign-language books which ought to be included in the libraries: "The wings between the towers called *Arctice* and *Cryere* contained rich libraries of Greek, Latin, Hebrew, French, Italian and Spanish volumes grouped in their respective sections" (*G*, 53). The significant additions here, Spanish and especially Italian, imply that the Thélèmites knew or were learning these languages. Rabelais opens up new vistas of learning and broadens the foundations of the new era. He deals here more forcefully with the question of the reading of Scriptures: "Here enter, all ye loyal scholars who expound/ Novel interpretations of the Holy Writ" (*G*, 54). Such Protestant interpretations can only be acquired from new translations or from a thorough knowledge of the original versions.

For the inhabitants of his abbey, Rabelais clearly delineates the moral aspects of education: the Thélèmites base their behavior on honor, virtue, and free will. In contrast to the letter to Pantagruel, one of the most noticeable innovations is the emphasis on physical activity; the Thélèmites can swim, ride horses, hunt or joust. On the theoretical level another step forward has been taken, though the transition must have been quite natural after describing Gargantua's education. In addition to whatever else the abbey of Thélème stands for, it represents an institution of learning and education, as in the case with all monasteries. However, it has its limitations; only the elite can enter it, and Rabelais has described an ideal institution. Although its practicality leaves much to be desired, it shows the changes in Rabelais's theory on education since the letter to Pantagruel.

II *From Unconsciousness to Consciousness*

Gargantua's education is presented in terms of contrast; Rabelais describes the medieval education in concrete terms, and extols the Renaissance pedagogy with effervescence and action which in turn ridicule the lethargy typical of the former. The narration of the giant's education, however, does more than indicate the cleavage between the old and the new; it achieves a higher artistic function because the style, closely orchestrated with the subject, is striking. At times the reader may be tempted to concentrate on the imagery or the characters for example, and consider them independently or show how they reinforce the meaning of the episode. The net result of this form of analysis proves again the superiority of *Gargantua* over *Pantagruel.*

In the first phase of Gargantua's education, Rabelais stresses the unconsciousness of his pupil; this state of mind, of course, coincides with the author's concept of the Middle Ages. He equates unconsciousness with the concrete. The giant neither acts nor reacts; he simply submits himself to the will of others; he is taught but does not himself learn. Rabelais illustrates with the image of stuffing someone who has no concern for assimilation or understanding. Gargantua goes through the motions of memorizing the basic medieval Latin textbooks dealing with grammar, religion and morals: the *Facet,* the *Ars Grammatica,* and the *Theodolet.* He loses all human characteristics and becomes an inert mass, a huge receptacle into which are poured fantastic amounts of disputable facts represented as concrete matter devoid of any spirituality. In listing the numerous books read to the giant, Rabelais produces a metaphor to express the feeding process: "and finally, other stuff of the same ilk, feather, kidney and broth. . . . Indeed, Gargantua grew as even as any down ever smoothed, as full of matter as any goose liver ever crammed!" (*G*, 14).

At this point in Gargantua's education we find ourselves in the realm of matter and not of the mind, very much like Dante's Hell. Since education usually deals with the spirit, this produces disdain and scorn of the scholastic pedagogical system. To underline the giant's animality, laziness, and helplessness, Rabelais stresses his base physiological functions which imply and compound the existing confusion and carelessness: "Next Gargantua dunged, piddled, vomited, belched, broke wind, yawned, spat, coughed, hiccoughed, sneezed and snotted himself as majestically and bountifully as an archdeacon" (*G*, 21). With the last simile,

Rabelais purposely throws the list of physiological activities into a religious, or scholastic, context; the derisive tone is heightened by the ironic adverbs.

Throughout the first phase, Rabelais transforms the spiritual, or abstract into the material, or concrete, by means of metaphors. Usually this sort of wilful transformation has the purpose of making a concept vivid so that the reader can grasp it more readily. Of course, the writer can express his admiration or scorn by choosing the metaphor from a more noble or vulgar plane than the topic at hand. Rabelais attains the realm of matter by sheer exaggeration, a logical means because of the gigantic setting, or by reducing the concrete to a low level: "Gargantua repaired to church with, in his train, a varlet bearing a basket. The latter contained a huge breviary swaddled in velvet and weighing about twelve hundred and six pounds including the filth of thumbmarks, dogeared corners. . . . Twenty-six or thirty masses ensued for the benefit of Gargantua and his chaplains. Under his tall hood, this chaplain looked like a peewit. . . . Chaplain and pupil babbled the mumbo jumbo of the litany, peeling [thumbing] their rosaries so carefully that not a single grain [bead] fell on the ground" (G, 21).

From Gargantua's lack of consciousness emerges an automatism in his action which enhances his wretched condition. Rabelais produces such a situation with a juxtaposition of activities which fuse the mental with the physical on a vulgar level: "Or with a deal of monkey chatter and head wagging (praying), he might go to look at some rabbit caught in a trap" (G, 22). In addition, to stressing his mechanical behavior, the author describes Gargantua with another image of stuffing which suggests the stoking of a furnace or boiler: "Then four servants in turn shovelled mustard in his mouth by the spadeful, thus preparing him to drain a horrific draught of white wine to relieve his kidneys" (G, 21).

The early *Gargantua* becomes an anachronism, when the general progressive and enlightened tone of the book is considered. The giant has been so perverted by his scholastic education that he is unaware of his ignorance; seen in this light he resembles Janotus de Bragmardo. Thus Rabelais arouses pity and not scorn for his giant. Gargantua's vegetating life then elicits compassion;

he is depicted as a creature slumbering in hibernation until the fertilizing spring sun begins to shine. Incessant sleep obviously symbolizes unconsciousness. The huge amount of food consumed by the giant should not shock anyone.[4] The exaggeration of the quantity, although befitting the gigantic scale, has a humorous effect on the episodes in which it occurs, but in this scholastic context it reinforces vulgar concreteness basic to the author's concept of medieval pedagogy. Of course, Rabelais exaggerates the faults of the medieval system in order to criticize and satirize, but there is much truth in his exposition. The filth of the educational institutions had become proverbial, and he alludes to it himself; as Gargantua combs out the cannon balls from his hair, his father asks him: "Upon my word, son, why have you brought us vermin hawks from the Collège de Montaigu?" (*G*, 37). According to documents, the students of that school went from prayer to memorization of knowledge and then to regurgitation of facts in meaningless debates that Rabelais also attacks.[5] The student began his day at four o'clock in the morning and was constantly kept busy until seven or eight o'clock in the evening with little time out for meals. To suit his satirical purposes Rabelais has Gargantua start his days under the old masters not before eight or nine o'clock in the morning.

The transition from the old to the new education occurs both on an antithetical and a grotesque level. To prove what the new education can accomplish, Rabelais introduces Eudemon, a twelve-year-old page destined to join Gargantua's retinue, who is the product of this system. The author leaves no doubt as to his attitude toward the young man by presenting us with a laudatory portrait of him: "He was so neat, so spruce, so handsome and his hair was so beautifully combed that he looked more like an angel than like a man" (*G*, 15). His behavior complements his physical appearance; he praises Gargantua for his knowledge, virtues, and manner and congratulates Grandgousier for giving his son such a good education. Although Eudemon's praise of his ruling lords appears to be in character, irony, heightened by the page's distinction and eloquence, prevails in the scene. The contrast between the two eras is shown in the following: "Gargantua's only reaction was to burst into tears. He bawled like a sick cow, hung his head and hid his face in his cap, until there was about as much possibility of drawing a word from him as a salvo of farts from the rump of a dead donkey." (*G*, 15). The two similes suffice to express the giant's condition. They easily transcend their vulgarity because they saliently describe Gargantua; through them we see a Gargantua who lives in an age blind to the piercing light. The medieval and grotesque colossus is thus opposed to the physically frail but intellectually sturdy boy.

Rabelais sees a complete cleavage between the Middle Ages and the Renaissance; as a result, a physician–scholar "purged Gargantua canonically with Anticyrian hellebore, an herb indicated for cerebral disorders and insanity, thus cleansing his brain of its unnatural, perverse condition" (*G*, 23). This second transition from the old to the new education, more abrupt than the first, marks the story's passing from one era to another. The purging episode in which Rabelais deals with medieval education for the last time contains grotesque and contrasting elements. Rabelais expresses the spiritual and the abstract in concrete physiological terms in order to sling a last muddy stone at the past. The adverb used to describe the purging process is worthy of attention; "canonically" enhances the grotesque purgation because of its various suggestive overtones. On the figurative level it means according to the canons, to the laws of purging; the metaphor fits in with the physician–scholar who administers the purge. Rabelais uses the word out of its usual context; he drastically lowers its usual meaning by applying the adverb to such a vulgar situation. On the other hand, the word remains in its proper plane since it directly refers to scholars; the ironic jab at scholasticism is indirect.

III   *A Feast of Words*

When the new era of education comes to the fore, a dam breaks in Rabelais's mind and waves of exuberance, energy, and enthusiasm come rushing through into his prose. The process is expressed in terms of action and movement now as if Rabelais could no longer contain his joy. Sainte-Beuve, the leading French critic of the nineteenth century, has made the most astute remarks on the subject: "French prose goes through its own gymnastics there, and style stands out prodigiously for its abundance, freedom, flexibility, both propriety and verve. Never had the

French language until that time experienced such a feast." [6] In this instance style not only reinforces and substantiates the meaning; it also has its own merit, proof of Rabelais's dexterous creativity. Significantly the description of Gargantua's physical activities occupies one of the longest chapters in his books. At this point the poetic vein came from a fertile source.

The most important innovation which Rabelais stresses in his system of education is physical activity of the body. In following this line of thought, he imitates the motto of antiquity: "Mens sana in corpore sano"—"a healthy mind in a healthy body"— but the motto becomes more than a principle or a practice; he incorporates it into his temperament and the essence of his art. Into the whirlpool of action, he pours a torrent of words; whenever the opportunity arises, he flashes his own creative motto: never one word when many will do the job better:

He proceeded to mount a fiery Italian charger, a Flemish dray horse, a Spanish jennet, an Arab thoroughbred and a hackney . . . Gargantua brandished the pike, plied the double-edged, two-handed sword, the bastard claymore used by archers, the Spanish rapier, the dagger and the poniard. . . . Gargantua also cast the dart, threw the iron bar, put the stone, tossed the boar spear, hurled the javelin, shied the halberd. . . . He could set a huge cannon on its carriage, hit buttmarks and other horizontal shooting, or, pointblank, bring down papgays [stuffed figures of parrots on poles], day pigeons and other verticle marks, facing them on a level or upwards or downwards or sidewise or backwards like the ancient Parthians . . . (G, 23).

In addition to military exercises, Gargantua indulges in all kinds of physical activity; swimming, climbing, singing, running, and shouting; however, the military exercises dominate because they suit the author's temperament better and lend themselves to more action. If these passages were dissected, immediately one would notice a dual structure: on the one hand, accumulations of nouns; on the other hand, accumulations of verbs. Both help to create the movement of the prose. The Diogenes episode of the third prologue comes to mind as one reads the description of the giant's activities; both episodes contain this dynamic expression of energy in which Rabelais excels.

Similes bring the giant down to an animal level: "He climbed trees like a cat, hopping from one to the next like a squirrel . . . he could scurry up the side of a house like a rat . . ." (G, 23). Although Rabelais stresses Gargantua's agility, he imparts some base features to his character by comparing him to a cat, a squirrel, or a rat. The common, and even vulgar, nature of the comparisons surpasses their original purpose. It necessitates a rapid readjustment which the mind cannot effect without some awareness of disproportion.

To express the joyful and carefree feeling which results from Gargantua's recent instruction, Rabelais adopts the present participle; the French suffix *ant* has a counterpart in the English *ing*. Much of the effect in the following passage results from the repetition of this part of speech: "Then they spent the whole day enjoying themselves to their heart's content, sporting and merrymaking, drinking toast for proffered toast, playing, singing, dancing, tumbling about, or loafing in some fair meadow, turning sparrows out of their nests, bagging quail and fishing for frogs and crayfish" (G, 24). In this sentence, one notices the trajectory which is projected by the various actions. At first the movement is moderately paced because of the irregular spacing of the participles; the climax is reached with the rapid succession of "playing, singing, dancing, tumbling," after which the cadence tapers off because one or more direct objects follow each participle.

Onomastics, the coining of names, provides Rabelais with a double-barrelled weapon to express his attitude toward education. Mocking Gargantua's first tutors, he forms vulgar names for them or whimsically fuses biblical names with theirs, thus insinuating additional criticism of scholasticism. The giant's first master is Tubal Holofernes; according to the Bible, Tubal, a descendant of Cain, invented the art of working metals; and Holofernes, of course, was the Babylonian general slain by Judith. The name Jobelin Bridé, or Jolter Clotpoll, Gargantua's second tutor, colloquially meant simpleton in Rabelais's day. On the other hand, the new teachers have names derived from Greek since they personify humanism; Ponocrates (powerful), Eudemon (fortunate), Anagnostes (reader), Theodore (God given) and Gymnaste (athlete). Onomastics forms an integral part of Rabelais's satire; in addition, it offers him an opportunity for verbal inventions, an outlet which he seeks constantly.

Whereas the first chapter, which deals with the Renaissance education, describes outdoor activities, the second one, much shorter in length, stresses observation rather than participation. On rainy days, supposedly, Gargantua goes out to observe various artisans and professionals at work; he will not grow up in an ivory tower but will have a global knowledge of society, its activities, and its ways of life. Rabelais also has his student acquaint himself with the plastic arts during this practical phase of his education. In other words, Gargantua participates in all aspects of human life; he wants to know theoretically or have a first-hand knowledge of everything. He represents truly the *uomo universale,* the "universal man" of the Renaissance.

Rabelais cannot claim to have instituted a completely novel pedagogy; his views contain some medieval features. He considerably depends on sheer memorization of an encyclopedic amount of facts. Rabelais puts Gargantua's words to Pantagruel into practice: "In sum, let me see an abyss of knowledge" (*P*, 8). Furthermore, like everything else transposed to this gigantic plane, the fantastic number of activities does not appear to be incongruous. Rabelais does not pretend to propose a workable program for every child; only his general methods are recommended. His student has a full schedule with absolutely no wasted time; he gets up at four o'clock in the morning, just like the students at the Collège de Montaigu. One must not forget, however, that Gargantua has much time for useful relaxation. The best illustration of some of the medieval features which remain occurs in the following scene: "Next, he would repair to secret places to make excretion of his natural digestion; here his tutor repeated what had been read, expounding its more obscure and difficult features" (*G*, 23). This in addition to the stuffed learning and the full use of time, is a perfect example of a contrast between the sublime and the vulgar, or between the spiritual and the physiological grotesque typical of the Middle Ages; it brings to mind the gargoyles on the cathedrals.

The scales tip, however, in favor of progress, of the Renaissance. Physical exercise, both for development and relaxation, is fea-

tured in the new approach. A certain freedom of action follows
many of the student's endeavors. Classical moderation in the
consumption of food marks the new spirit. Body hygiene is introduced into daily life. One of Gargantua's more modern interests
is his affinity for inventing and producing motorized objects;
Leonardo da Vinci, of course, paved the way somewhat earlier.
Many of Rabelais's fundamental pedagogical theories will recur
later in Rousseau's *Emile*. He believes, for example, that the
student must have a natural inclination toward learning; the
student must not be compelled. Therefore, the teacher should
present the subject matter to the student in a pleasant fashion.
Nature is one of the best educative guides; Rousseau's back-to-
nature thesis has a counterpart in Gargantua's visits to the artisans
to observe daily living. Gargantua's learning of astronomy by
close observation of the beauties of the heavens reminds one of
Emile's similar experience.

If Rabelais can be considered an innovator in pedagogical
matters, he certainly would not claim orginality in the field. He
sides with many other humanists who favored reform. In one
case he might easily have known a work written as early as 1260
by an Italian scholarly physician which deals with the importance
of physical exercise and hygiene, Taddeo Alderotti's *Della Con-
servazione della salute*. In the fifteenth century other Italians,
namely Pier Paolo Vergerio and Maffio Vegio wrote treatises on
education. The list broadens in the sixteenth century; both Baltazar Castiglione's *Courtier* and Erasmus' dissertations criticize the
poor quality of instruction. Sir Thomas More joins the fray, and
two Germans, Ulrich de Hutten and Melanchton, both active in
the Reformation movement, attack the teaching manuals and
methods. Another renowned figure in the Renaissance pedagogical world is the Spanish Luis Vivès who studied in Paris and in
1531 published his *De Disciplinis*.[7] Nevertheless, one cannot deny
the fact that Rabelais brings revolutionary pedagogical methods
to the French scene.

A discussion of Rabelais's system of education necessitates a
confrontation with Montaigne, author of the philosophical *Essays*,
and the other leading prose writer of the latter part of the sixteenth century.[8] In his essay "Of Children's Education" (Book
I, Chapter 26), Montaigne proposes an instruction based on se-

lected subjects in which assimilation matters more than quantity. His goal is a well-bred, genteel, and sophisticated gentleman who will impress but not stagger society. Traditionally it is said that Rabelais advocates *la tête bien pleine,* "a mind stuffed with information"; whereas Montaigne suggests *la tête bien faite,* "the well-bred mind." Rabelais's attitude cannot be considered a fault. An unquenched thirst for knowledge marked his times; fifty years later Montaigne could well afford to take a moderate stand. The fact that Rabelais's Thélèmites represent Montaigne's brand of education has been overlooked.

IV *Cicero Through the Rabelaisian Lens*

Many of Rabelais's views on ethics and education appear in his letters or speeches. These are written in contrived prose, highly rhetorical in tone. In these instances, Rabelais shows another aspect of humanism; he indulges in a favorite pastime of the humanists who abused the ciceronian model and, like himself, regarded the form as an exercise in rhetoric. In dealing with the Picrocholine war, Rabelais conveys some of his ethical notions in two separate addresses. The first one, given by Gallet, Grandgousier's legal counsel, fits in with the character of the emissary and for once gives a positive view of the profession's jargon. It attacks what one would term today unprovoked aggression. Structurally, the speech follows the pattern established by Cicero: a direct exordium, or beginning of speech, composed of majestic sentences to attract the audience's attention; the narration of the fact, in long sentences punctuated by repetitions; the arguments, expounded through rhetorical questions, and finally a vigorous and vehement peroration, or ending.

According to Gallet's oration, reason and fear of God constitute the main guidelines for human behavior and form the ingredients of judgment: "The whole thing is so unreasonable, so contrary to good sense as to defy all human understanding. No stranger will credit it until the outcome proves that all we hold sacred and holy abandons such a breakaway from God and Reason to woo their own depraved inclinations" (*G*, 31). In other words, Rabelais advocates a fusion of the rational and emotive feelings which will lead to moderation, the ideal of antiquity. However, he cannot completely sustain the ennobling tone of the address; in typical fashion, it degenerates at the end into vulgarity with the naming of Picrochole's henchmen as hostages and produces the recurring contrast between the sublime and the vulgar: "But you must leave as hostages the Dukes of Tournemoule, Basde-fesses, Merdail, the Prince of Gratelles and the vicomte de Mor-piaille, or, as we know them, my Lords Twiddlemussle, Low-buttock, Smalltittle, Scratchballock and Diddlesnoop" (*G*, 31).

In Gargantua's address to Pirochole's defeated soldiers, Rabelais advocates kindness, consideration, and forgiveness as additional components of his moral system of education. In keeping with his character, Gargantua's language is less formal than Gallet's. The giant has evolved from the beginning of the book, has gained maturity and wisdom, and now appears as a benevolent monarch who instead of punishing his enemies believes in rehabilitating them to a peaceful life: "Time which mines and corrupts all other things on earth unfailingly increases and augments men's bene-factions. A generous deed done to a man of reason grows con-stantly by human appreciation and remembrance" (*G*, 50). In this particular passage, the rhetorical tone derives from the fre-quent use of synonymous pairs of words. The implication in Gargantua's speech is that the victor should not trample the vanquished and disregard his human dignity for fear of later reprisals and revenge, an ancient notion which Montaigne stressed in his essays "The Cannibals." As in the preceding speech, Rabe-lais cannot keep a straight face throughout; he has to insinuate some disparaging remarks. At one point, as he describes what some vanquished people gave in tribute to their conqueror, the enumeration deteriorates from the noble to the vulgar: "The crowds thronged about his ships, tossing into them all they held precious: gold, silver, rugs, jewels, spices, drugs, aromatics, par-rots, pelicans, monkeys, civets, genets and porcupines" (*G*, 50).

All of Rabelais's ideas about intellectual and moral education may not please the modern reader, especially the young ones. In the *Third Book*, he devotes a strongly worded chapter entirely (Chapter 48) to the question of marriage without parental con-sent; he vehemently deplores the fact that many young persons elope and are helped in this foul endeavor by the priests who see the opportunity to assert their power over the lives of individ-uals. Gargantua advises his son to go on his trip in search of the

Divine Bottle; upon his return he will have a wife and all the wedding plans arranged for him. Pantagruel respectfully submits himself to the will of his father. At first sight, such attitudes may appear archaic, but Rabelais's reasoning goes beyond the parent-child relationship. His vehemence in the matter results from his deep feelings concerning the overextended worldly powers of the Church.

To give his convictions the fervor they deserve, Rabelais uses a rhetorical prose which hammers and pounds feeling into some of his ideas. He achieves this effect through the alignment of synonyms; thus, each additional synonym is heightened by the pitch of his anger. Style here reinforces content. Rabelais maneuvers his prose carefully and employs the synonyms to great advantage, producing a variety of structural parallelisms. At times, he will proceed by groups of three: "No law ever I heard of, sacred, profane or barbarous justified children in marrying according to their will, without seeking the advice, consent and approval of their fathers, mothers, and near relatives" (III, 48). He likes to create antitheses, here between evil and good, the abductor and the maiden. The two-to-one ratio between the dominant synonyms for villain and the subordinated maiden, give the impression of the girl's helplessness: "Take the most arrogant ruffian, villain or scoundrel; the most evil smelling, foul-breathing hangdog; the most scurvy and leprous stinkard; the most vicious footpad or brigand imaginable. Well such knave may abduct the most highborn, the richest, the most upright and the chastest maiden in the land" (III, 48); "And the woeful fathers and mothers seeing abducted and taken away from their houses by a completely rotten, cancrous, cadaverous, poor and unfortunate, unkown man, stranger, barbarian, rascal so beautiful, delicate, rich and healthy daughter . . ." (III, 48). In the last example there is a double chiasmus, one of contrast between the man and the woman, and a complementary one in the description of the man himself between the nouns and the adjectives. One notices as well an interior arrangement within the list of synonyms by groups of two: unknown man-stranger, barbarian-rascal, rotten, cancrous and cadaverous leading to poor and unfortunate.

A final group of parallelisms, instead of this balanced effect, conveys a notion of progression: "Yet never a clause, paragraph, point or title in the body of natural, international or imperial law prescribed penalty or torture for such an act" (III, 48). The first group of synonyms is a list of diminishing proportions, whereas within the second, space widens; consequently, Rabelais produces a contrast of space between the descending and ascending progressions which by their very definition produce a movement of the prose, as is the case in the use of all other groups of synonyms. Style is inseparable from idea; it reinforces and even dominates content occasionally. Rabelais the artist always looms in the background.

A study of Rabelais's concept of intellectual, moral, and physical education reveals an ideological and stylistic fusion of antiquity, the Middle Ages, and the Renaissance. He cannot claim originality of thought, but he sums up the past and the present, and, along certain pedagogical lines, announces the future. His verve breaks through at every opportunity and gives an even greater significance to his ideas in the form of an exuberant or a carefully contrived style. In analyzing education in Rabelais's works, we transcend the philosophical and are able to determine the tenor of the work as a whole from a particular vantage point.

CHAPTER 7

Apparent Rhetoric and Lasting Esthetics

HAVING been a monk for at least thirty years during a period of religious ferment, Rabelais could not very well have avoided the question of God. Like other humanists, the new protesting religion attracted him, especially since he had disposed of his monastic garb for the more secular priestly robe. Eventually his personal religion must have transcended the limitations of Catholicism or Protestantism and incorporated some Pantagruelism, his own philosophy of life—if it can be considered as such.

In a dedicatory poem which precedes the prologue to *Pantagruel,* Hughes Salel, a contemporary poet, compliments Rabelais for pursuing "progress behind your quips and repartees." In the famous prologue to *Gargantua,* Rabelais himself urges the reader to break the marrow bone and extract the hidden meaning. Are these incitements serious or in jest? Most critics have taken the bait and swallowed them without much hesitation. They have classified Rabelais in almost every area of the religious spectrum, atheistic, Catholic, and finally Protestant. These classifications offer no really new choice. More than one hundred years ago Sainte-Beuve had the correct outlook in deriding them all: "When one tries to pull Rabelais in one direction, he lets one do it and . . . he goes there, but he laughs at it. He must be surprised to have become in form of a legend, an apostle, a saint, a future Evangelistic Christ.[1]

I *Faith, Reason, and Naturalism*

At the turn of the century, studies on the author of *Gargantua* gained new impetus under the leadership of Abel Lefranc, who directed the monumental unfinished critical edition, and transformed Rabelais into a mocking atheist. He derives most of the allegations to substantiate this conclusion from *Pantagruel*. To begin with, Lefranc cites Pantagruel's genealogy (*P, 2*) which in his eyes parodies Christ's genealogy given in the Bible; Rabelais even uses the biblical "begat." In the same chapter, the picture of the giant Hurtaly straddling Noah's ark is a striking travesty of the Flood. Gargantua's letter to Pantagruel best proves Rabelais's lack of religion. At one point, the giant-father tells his son: "When, by His pleasure, which rules and orders everything, my soul must abandon this human habitation, I shall not believe I am dying utterly, but rather passing from one place to another" (*P, 8*). This "dying utterly," along with other specific phrases would indicate Rabelais's disbelief in the immortality of the soul; immortality is achieved instead through one's descendants. Panurge's trick on the priest who, as he takes off his ceremonial garb before the congregation finds himself without clothes, might be proof of Rabelais's rash irreverence, but the medieval *fabliaux* were full of such tales.

On another occasion, Panurge's vulgar prank on a Parisian woman who finds herself followed by thousands of dogs in heat, would be to deride the Corpus Christi processions. Pantagruel's prayer preceding the grotesque conflict with Werewolf is most inopportune; it indicates Rabelais's scornful disregard for prayers. In addition, the "Hoc fac et vinces" heard from Heaven by Pantagruel (an allusion to Constantine's hearing "In hoc signo vinces" before he captured Rome and forced Christianity on the heathen Goths) would supposedly be intended to downgrade, if not satirize, the emperor's miraculous experience. Furthermore, Panurge's resurrection of the beheaded Epistemon parodies Christ's miracles. Finally, Rabelais's description of popes' menial occupations in Hell casts a dark satirical shadow over the pontificate and the Church, but, with such criterion, Dante too would have to be considered an anti-Catholic or atheist.[2]

Lefranc points out the giant's unusual birth through his mother's ear in *Gargantua*, and sees in this incident a mocking allusion to Christ's miraculous birth, although such extraordinary births have a long tradition in the epics of antiquity. In the fantastic dialogues of Chapter 5, to which we shall return, one of the characters, a cleric, at one point utters, "Sitio" ("I am thirsty"), one of Christ's last words on the cross. Lefranc considers this

utterance a most explicit blasphemy on the name of Jesus and another indication of Rabelais's free thinking. It has been pointed
out, however, that such remarks on the part of monks or other
ecclesiastical men were not particularly shocking and belonged
to an array of "professional" puns.[3] Although solid refutations
soon appeared on the scene, Lefranc's position continued to find
adherents until just a few years ago.[4]

Re-evaluations of the question lead to the conclusion that
Rabelais was as good a Catholic as many of his contemporaries.[5]
In the case of Gargantua's letter to Pantagruel, a leading scholar
cites St. Paul, St. Thomas, and St. Bonaventure to show that the
document does not contain any trace of heresy; he even juxtaposes
passages from the letter and from the Scriptures which clearly
bear out the fact that Rabelais paraphrases them.[6] Accordingly,
the famous enigma surrounding Rabelais's thought has no validity.[7] Lefranc has merely distorted the texts to make them fit his
thesis that Rabelais is an atheist. For instance, Lefranc contends
that Epistemon's resurrection parodies Lazarus' and Jairus' resur-
rections by Christ. In a most important study on the question of
Rabelais's religion, one scholar has successfully proven instead
that the author has in mind a medieval epic *Les Quatre fils
Aymon* or *The Four Sons Aymon* which he himself mentions in
the prologue to *Pantagruel*. In this tale, Richard, one of the characters, is revived by Maugis, a magician, who sews up the wound
and, after having applied an ointment to it, gives him a good
dose of wine. Moreover, the situation of miraculous healings or
resuscitations belongs to a long literary tradition beginning with
the Classical epics. Rabelais might have had the Bible in mind,
but not primarily; on the contrary, the episode with Epistemon,
an imitation of a scene from a romance of chivalry and not a
biblical incident, forms an integral part of the parody of the epic
which dominates so much of Pantagruel.[8]

The pendulum, having swung from one side to the other, is
now wrested from its usual course finding itself pointing toward
Protestantism. Lefranc had already alluded to Rabelais's tenden-
cies toward the reforming thought. He points out that, unlike
the usual monastery, there is no church in the abbey of Thélème,
but that there are individual praying parlors.[9] A more credible
argument for Rabelais's evangelism could be that only worshipers

of the unadulterated Gospels are admitted to the abbey. Grand-gousier addresses himself directly to God without the intercession of saints or the Virgin. The frequent references to St. Paul, the reformers' apostle and evangelical purist, could easily substantiate the idea that there was a reformist phase in Rabelais's thought around 1534. His scathing attacks on the useless monks and his condemnation of pilgrimages, although in a reformist vein, have distinct antecedents in the Middle Ages and in his contemporary, Erasmus.

Although Lefranc's rational thesis has been refuted, it has the dubious distinction of having started a series of arguments and confrontations which would have delighted Rabelais himself. First, the very examples used to view Rabelais as an atheist boomeranged to show him a Catholic; now, after Lefranc's death, the cannonade continues, but to establish Rabelais as an evangelist on the basis of the same episodes. The birth of Gargantua through his mother's ear, in this latter view, no longer parodies Christ's miraculous birth, but upholds the dogma of faith and reliance on God, and thus indicates that nothing is impossible for Him. It is pointed out that such dogmatic notions fall into the Lutheran interpretation of the Bible.[10] The "Hoc fac et vinces" heard by Pantagruel before battling Werewolf it is claimed derives directly from St. Luke (III, 22) "Hoc fact et vives." The misquotation by Rabelais receives slight attention. The citation supposedly conveys the idea of free will and is used to support the thesis concerning Rabelais's orthodoxy in interpreting and explicating the Bible. This notion of free will with all its Lutheran overtones but with medieval roots as well, emerges fully in the abbey of Thélème. By "Hoc fac et vinces," Rabelais also means preach the Gospel, a leading protestant innovation, and devide the law according to Christian interpretation.[11] Other episodes following this line of thought outside of the Lefranc realm further expose an evangelical Rabelais. The Tale of Puddingballocks and his ax is an example of the author's belief in Calvinist predestination[12]—and the whole *Third Book* can be seen in this same light, because Panurge is predestined to failure. Stoutmoron and his worship of the Decretals reflects the reformists' strong feelings against the concept of a God on earth, the pope.

The latest conclusion suggests that Rabelais envisaged religious reforms along Anglican lines and would have found himself most at home in the Church of England. With this last approach, the re-evaluation of Rabelais's religion has completed its cycle; he has had placed upon him all of the main beliefs of Western Christianity and by implication Hebrew and Classical religious teachings. We hope that since the reader has such a variety of choice, matters of religion can henceforth be laid to rest. The fact that Rabelais fits into so many theological categories may imply that he supersedes them all.

The general consensus of opinion maintains, and rightly so, that Rabelais has faith.[13] In the prologue to the *Fourth Book,* which gives a serious indication of Rabelais's thoughts on the matter a year before his death, he explicitly states his reverence and belief in God: "Such is the will of the mighty, beneficent and omnipotent Creator, whom I acknowledge and obey. Whose sacrosanct and auspicious Word I revere. (By Word, I mean Bible)." In the same book, he explicitly affirms the immortality of the soul: "All intellectual souls, I think, are exempt from the scissors of the cruel Fate, Atropos [death]. . . . They are all immortal, be they angelic, demonic or human" (IV, 27). The famous episode that follows, the description of the Greek god Pan, equated with Christ, brings out a strong sense of Christian faith. The reaction of Pantagruel, Rabelais's mouthpiece, is especially noteworthy: "God may perfectly be called, in the Greek tongue, Pan, which means 'All.' All that we are, all that we live, all that we hope is Himself, in Him, from Him and by Him. He is the Good Pan, the supreme Shepherd . . . all-merciful Pan, our one and only Saviour, died near Jerusalem in the reign of Tiberius Caesar. His story told, Pantagruel relapsed into profound silence, lost in his own thoughts. Shortly after we noticed tears dropping from his eyes . . ." (IV, 28).

Whether Rabelais would fit into one given Christian sect or another remains quite conjectural and somewhat inconsequential. Lefranc's theory was founded largely on judgments by sixteenth-century contemporaries of Rabelais who regarded him as an atheist.[14] During the period of time, anyone who did not agree with the prevalent or accepted Church dogmas automatically fell into the free-thinking category. Despite its gravity and the resulting death penalty, such a verdict was readily passed by one individual on another, often out of sheer pettiness; consequently, these early judgments have limited validity and certainly lack objectivity. One fact remains indubitable: Rabelais steers away from extremes, Protestant or Catholic. He has momentary Lutheran or even Calvinist learnings, but backs away as soon as they become doctrinaire. Rabelais's books form a receptacle for all ideas which preoccupied his times, but they don't necessarily express his own views; one must beware of taking everything found in his works literally. Some notions occur strictly because of the exigencies of the text, or to bring about some comic effect. Rabelais knew the Bible well; and the frequency of Scriptural quotes or paraphrases, to a great extent from St. Paul, might indicate a leaning toward the purist views of this apostle, but we cannot transform these into a religious system.

Rabelais juxtaposes ideas as they present themselves to him, without any organization. His mind works by association; many ideas found in his works reflect what his contemporary readers wanted to read or discuss, rather than his own convictions. In the final analysis, Rabelais is not a rationalist, but he is rational in his approach to religion. He always chooses the golden mean; he reads the Bible for himself, and does not accept the interpretations of others. The essence of what he reads in the Scriptures is shown in the universality of his ethical and moral code.

In a parable in the *Fourth Book* (Chapter 31), Rabelais hints strongly at his convictions concerning the rational against the irrational and the perverted. Pantagruel, who continues his role as the man of common sense and wisdom, narrates the fable of Physis and Antiphysis. Significantly enough, the fable never reaches the full development of the ones about Master Gaster, King Lent, or the Chitterlings. It remains on an abstract level, probably because Rabelais wants to stress its didactic purposes. If it were expanded like the others, its artistic features would then dominate the ideas. As already indicated, Rabelais borrowed the fable from the Italian Ferrarese, Caelius Calcagnini, who in 1544 had published it in his *Gigantes* (See Chapter 4, note 1.). Rabelais only used it to convey a definite point: his opposition, if not anger, at false distortions of religion and misinterpretations of his books. Physis represents Nature, Beauty and Harmony; Antiphysis, Nature's opposite, in turn begat *Amo-*

dunt ("formlessness") and Dissonance or Confusion. Irony prevails as Antiphysis is praised as a perfect creation; her children

boast of spherical heads and feet, to walk wheeling circularly, whereas Physis' offsprings are deformed. Because of her "perfection" Antiphysis brought all the numbskulls and crackpots to her opinion, and because the subject of the admiration of a host of brainless idiots. Since then she has begotten the hypocritical dissemblers, the swiveling sham-Abrahams and popemongers . . . the maniac bigots and blowhards . . . the demoniacal and Calvinist impostors of Geneva . . . the insane acolytes of Gabriel de Puy-Herbault, that monk bigot of Tontevrault, who cries scandal at honest books [Rabelais's] . . . the gormandizing beggar-priests . . . the dunces of the cowl . . . the Phariser shufflers, the hooded pinchbacks and all manner of other formless ill-favored monsters, fashioned in spite of Nature . . .(IV, 32).

If one follows nature, the path will take a reasonable course. Rabelais considers this form of naturalism when he expounds the part of his philosophy of life; that is Pantagruelism. Much has been said about Pantagruelism; some have even claimed that it is the basis of Rabelais's thought. Looking at the text, however, we notice definitions of Pantagruelism occur only three different times, totaling four or five lines, in addition to a few other indirect allusions to it. Such a sparse exposition warrants caution if one who would try to expand it and make it embrace the work as a whole. In these instances, Rabelais without a doubt meant what he said, but Pantagruelism cannot consequently be transformed into an elaborate system of thought. Its importance should not be overestimated; any such attempt distorts the text.

In the evaluation of Rabelais's thought, one gets the impression of rapacious birds anxiously awaiting the appearance of a mite in order to pounce upon it. The first definition of Pantagruelism appears in *Pantagruel:* "live peaceful, happy, healthy and forever content" (I, 34). The striking note of optimism in this advice relates more, perhaps, to the tone of the book than to practicality. It represents an idealization, just like the abbey of Thélème's motto "Do as you will." What emanates from this bit of thought is an earthy enthusiasm for life, certainly a dominant motif in Rabelais's works.

The second fractured, stylized, and oblique definition of Pantagruelism appears in the prologue to the *Third Book*, "For in my readers I discern the same specific force that our ancestors called Pantagruelism. Thanks to this personal property, they cannot misunderstand anything born of a good, free and loyal heart." Although a trace of pessimism infiltrates the earlier optimism, it continues to dominate; there will be adversities to overcome, but good will prevail. In keeping with the tone of the *Third Book*, this Pantagruelism reaches a higher and more abstract level of meaning; it does not supplant the earlier version but complements it.

The final version occurs in the prologue to the *Fourth Book;* as in the preceding book, it restates the definition, but in explicit and full terms. As a matter of fact it gives the only true definition. Oddly enough, though, Rabelais inserts it in parentheses, probably to minimize its importance: "a certain gaiety of spirit produced by a contempt of the incidentals of fate."

Running parallel to the progressive refinement of Rabelais's works is the evolution of his philosophy of life from a seemingly carefree and bursting love for earthly existence and its pleasures (actually a moderate form of Epicureanism), to a kind of stoicism. Such an about-face should not surprise us, because twenty years separate these two attitudes. Rabelais's faltering health in 1552 is a cause of the change, and we see his preoccupation with such matters in the prologue to the *Fourth Book;* even in the prologue to the *Third Book*, in the Diogenes episode, some stoic and cynical elements have taken on notable importance. Pantagruel's behavior in the last two books is that of a stoic character; his apathy, meditation and cultivation of his own virtue cast him in this light. However, Rabelais's religious vein cannot allow stoicism to dominate.[15]

In the kaleidoscope of Rabelais's thought, neoplatonism occupies a sizable space; to what extent he really believes in it or is merely following a vogue of his times remains highly conjectural.[16] Of significance along this line of thought is the *dizain,* the ten-line poem, which precedes the *Third Book.* It is dedicated to Marguerite, Queen of Navarre, author of a series of tales which Boccaccio inspired called the *Heptameron,* and of some contemplative poetry which expresses her spiritual struggle to reconcile Platonism and Christianity. In the dizain, he admonishes the queen to leave the lofty and edifying realm of her soul's pre-occupation and come back to earthly matters:

> You have, O royal Soul, without regret
> Fled softly from your mortal habitation
> (Your comely body which was ever set
> On doing your will here in its earthly station).
> In heaven, your element, your inchoation,
> You are content . . . Yet let a kindly fate
> Restore you to our midst, compassionate,
> Making your eyes to range, your thoughts to dwell
> On this, which is the third book to relate
> The Joyous Feats of Good Pantagruel.

The fact that Rabelais dedicates the *Third Book* to the Queen of Navarre implies much more than a mere respectful gesture on his part toward the leading lady of France; he invites her to read his book because she will find in it the spiritual food for her soul which she has been seeking. She will not, however, find a better solution in Rabelais's books than in her own search. She sought to leave the material world and live in the spiritual realm of complete immersion in God. This ideal state of life leads to an ascetic existence and the eventual breakdown of the individual, which proves the inadvisability of this search for the ideal. Panurge starts on the quest for his ideal of happiness and self-knowledge, but in the process Panurge instead acquires "philautie," or self-love. His failure ought to indicate to the queen that her own path toward the Platonic Ideal, the eventual spiritual union of man and God, will reap the same disastrous and perverted rewards.

Trying to bring Rabelais's thought and religion down to a common denominator will meet with failure. His works resemble a kaleidoscope which, as it turns, offers a variety of designs; not one specifically represents Rabelais, but their composite framework approximates his ideas. His books are best described as an anatomy—namely, all the parts are needed to make the whole, and no particular limb should be stretched in favor of another, for fear of distorting the body. Above all, the reader has to bear in mind that the passages which explicitly state Rabelais's ideas form a small segment of all the books. If one places too much emphasis on the rhetorical parts, the dominant creative and artistic portions will wrongfully suffer and be relegated to the background, as so often happens.

II *Obsession Transformed into Art*

Sometimes a person writes because he finds himself so obsessed by certain thoughts or observations on life that he feels compelled to express them for his contemporaries and for posterity. His writing then acts as a form of catharsis for himself and sometimes for the reader as well. If he would reach greatness, the rhetorical content of his work has to be suffused with imagination and artistry; otherwise, instead of imaginative and creative literature, we have journalism, pamphlet writing, sociology, or history.

Without doubt, many things preyed on Rabelais's mind: the abuses of the Church, its scholastic and theologically biased domination of cultural life, the waste and uselessness of the vast monastic empire, the quest for peace in the midst of turbulent spiritual and political climate, the search for new values in life through reconciling ancient philosophical patterns (stoicism, Epicureanism, Platonism, Pyrrhonism, materialism, etc.) with the old and the new Christianity. Seen in his time, Rabelais then belongs to a long list of sixteenth-century personalities who expounded the same ideas. He let his obsessions weigh on him until he began to write at the age of forty, a relatively late start for a man of letters, and his creative period lasted only twenty years. But he had the capability and the imagination to place these bothersome demons into a fictional wrapping so that his books live on.

Rabelais created his own universe, one constantly renewing itself, in which his imagination deployed itself freely. A singular compulsion occurs in the creative process; once Rabelais has given birth to his creations, they repeatedly attract him back to them. He finds solace in his created universe which often has more reality and meaning than the world about him. Extracted from time and space, characters assume more validity than the reality which gives them a basis for life. Panurge, Gargantua, Pantagruel, Friar John, Janotus de Bragmardo, Bridlegoose, and a host of others fall into this category of characters who are fixed in eternity. Art becomes the creator's religion—what he believes in sincerely and finds irrefutable. He makes himself and Man eternal through creativity, for art supersedes and outlives Man. This is Rabelais. In the midst of a religiously torn world which aimed at stability, he found spiritual tranquillity and peace of mind in the creation of a universe of fantasy ruled by intellectual, physical, and verbal activity. Because he repeatedly came back to his basic set of characters, though changing them, he felt this compulsive creative urge grip him time and time again, in addition to the need he felt to plunge himself into the ideological quarrels of his day. He certainly hoped that long after the religious, political, and philosophical debates would belong to history, *Gargantua* and *Pantagruel* would continue to rank among the genial contributions to world culture. These books are not mere vehicles for ideas; they give evidence of painstaking artistic work on Rabelais's part. The impression of rambling and disorganized characterization, verbal accumulations, and meaningless successions of episodes rapidly fades upon closer investigation. Each episode represents an autonomous unit to be judged independently as well as in relation to others. The assembled components form a sparkling *collage* which bears strong resemblance in technique and in spirit to Joyce's works. Logical concepts of time and space are broken down; the power of the word reigns supreme.

The fifth chapter of *Gargantua,* the "Palaver of the Potulent," or as Rabelais calls it "Conversations of the well-inebriated," gives excellent evidence of Rabelais's art, his verbal and spiritual exuberance. This scene discovers an assemblage of individuals representing a cross-section of society gaily awaiting Gargantua's birth; in the meantime they engage in a series of lengthy, lively, and carefree comments:

> Our fathers drank lustily and emptied their pots!
> Well hummed, well bummed: a fine movement of music and
> bowels. Now let us drink up!
> This round will wash your guts for you! Have you anything
> to send to the river? That's where tripe is washed: give
> this drink your message!
> I drink no more than a sponge!
> I drink like a Knight Templar.

Spongia, a sponge, eh? Well, I drink *tanquam sponsus,* like
a bridegroom.
And I *sicut terra sine aqua,* like earth without water.
Give me a synonym of the word 'ham'!
A subpoena served upon thirst; a compulsory instrument in
the jurisprudence of drinking. A pulley, too: you use a
pulley to get your wine down into the cellar, and ham to
get it down into your belly (*G,* 5).

Here, in essence, is the spirit of Rabelais; he plunges us in
the midst of his effervescent imagination by means of lively
dialogues and wordplay, all alive with movement and action, his
favorite domain. With an allusive repartee, he constructs his
dramatis personae. We guess through the dialogue the identity
of the individuals: a soldier, a cleric, a priest, a servant, a lawyer,
or a farmer. This impressionistic technique results in a juxtaposition of dialogues in the same vein as the French contemporary
new novel. The quick succession of short retorts animates the
scene and their accumulation conveys the feeling of words spoken
for the sheer pleasure of the participants and the audience. The
episode then takes on a gratuitous quality, the result of a fecund
outburst of fantasy, and the words become poetry or vehicles for
image, play with sounds, and meaning. Consequently, the episode
reflects the tone and the purpose of a major portion of Rabelais's
books: an artistic exercise and creation which we admire for its
esthetic qualities and whose charm we experience, as if before
a painting.

CHAPTER 8

Conclusion

G IGANTICISM, epic tradition, the Quarrel of Women, and imaginary voyages form only the framework of Rabelais's books because he then proceeds to fill out the canvas with his original characters and episodes and injects into it his own fluid ideas on a number of subjects close to his contemporaries. But, above all, this framework constitutes a deep receptacle which he fills to overflowing capacity with his boundless fantasy.

With each succeeding book, the link between the narrative or the oral tradition, and the development of the action become more tenuous. Gradually Rabelais's imagination needs only the slightest support before it is able to assert itself fully. The creative leap from *Pantagruel* to *Gargantua* is a good indication of the craftsman's progress. Giganticism, for example, frees itself from its earlier material form and acquires a satirical as well as an intrinsic role; it becomes the very spirit of the Renaissance and the very essence of the narrative technique—a source of tales and imagery; it will occur under one form or another in all books. Rabelais has to inflate everything he deals with on a thematic or verbal level; his exuberance dictates such a procedure. As a result, the epic tradition is soon engulfed by the sprawling tentacles of an expansive imagination.

The *Third Book* and the *Fourth Book* rapidly surpass their apparent scope, whether it is the Quarrel of Women or the question of marriage in the former, or the tales of adventurous and fantastic voyages in the latter. If a case can be made for the interpretation of the *Third Book* as a quest for happiness or self-knowledge, the dominating feature of the book remains the succession of theatrical scenes producing a taunting comedy composed of dynamic vignettes. The search for a unifying theme can result in neglecting the value of the parts not only in the *Third*

Book but in the *Fourth Book* as well. In the latter the fragmentation is all the more evident due to the lack of a dense jelling compound, except the superficial hunt for the Divine Bottle. Each episode has to be judged on its own merits; then a whimsical universe emerges inhabited by amorphic surrealistic beings, children of a creative imagination.

In an effort to further the rehabilitation of the prologues, this study has viewed them as microcosms of the books they precede; in addition, they gain another dimension when judged in relationship to each other because they dramatize the creative evolution of the books themselves. They can no longer be considered as obstacles before the principal attraction. Formerly they were important, as in *Gargantua* or in the *Third Book,* only if they carried some hidden or esoteric *meaning;* to evaluate them only as abstracted capsules of ideas hardly suffices.

What direction should Rabelais studies take? Until now, critics have tried to extract an ideological "substantific marrow." As a result many interpretations have not only enlightened but sometimes also distorted the text; however, the availability of additional marrows is rapidly coming to an end. Will the belief that Rabelais is a Catholic, atheist, Episcopalian (unknown to him), stoic, or rationalist enhance our knowledge of him as a writer of literature, that is, as a contributor to one of the art forms? One wonders how this variety of meanings enlightens the modern reader and what relationship exists between such interpretations and the literary value of the text. It is true, however, that the controversy over the meaning of Rabelais's books created in the Renaissance had greater validity at that time than now. On the other hand, Rabelais's humanism, which was a rediscovery of ethical and religious values derived from the ancients, reflects that of many of his contemporaries.

But the humanist also transmits and worships knowledge and the creativity of the mind. Although it expounds and implies some ideas, Rabelais's mind has produced a universe of creations that live not only by the power of their physical action but mostly by the overflowing dynamism of their verbal activity; and Rabelais himself participates in this last activity, thus becoming one of the contributing characters. Herein lies the essence of his books. To those who will object that verbal dexterity, a sweeping imagination, and an abounding creative spirit do not suffice to arrive at the lasting ingredients of literature, the answer is that these elements give literature most of its transcendental life.

Notes and References

Chapter One

1. François Rabelais, *Pantagruel*, ed. Abel Lefranc, III (Paris, 1922), xiv–xviii.

2. Lefranc solidified the notion of a Rabelais parodying the Bible (*ibid.*, pp. xlii–lii) but this thesis was soon contradicted by Lucien Febvre, *Le Problème de l'incroyance au XVIe siècle. La Religion de Rabelais* (Paris, 1942).

3. This enumeration of giants brings to mind Hugo's similar enterprise at the beginning of *La Légende des siècles*. The poet was a fervent admirer of Rabelais and felt a genuine affinity of spirit for his literary ancestor; cf. my *Etude sur le comique de Rabelais* (Florence, 1964), pp. 101–02.

4. K. H. Francis, "Rabelais and Mathematics," *Bibliothèque d'Humanisme et Renaissance*, XXI (1959), 95–96.

5. Lefranc in his introduction to the critical edition of *Pantagruel* views this scene as an example of Rabelais's parodying Christ's miracles. This matter, placed in a broader context, will be discussed at length in the last chapter.

6. The opinions regarding this episode vary, contradict, and yet complement each other. It is considered a parody of student verbiage (R. Sturel "La Prose poétique au XVIe siècle," *Mélanges Lanson* [Paris, 1922, pp. 47–60], a means for Rabelais to be eloquent and enrich the French language (V.-L. Saulnier, "L'Ecolier limousin," *Revue des Cours et des Conférences*, XL [1939] 307) and a strictly gratuitous scene aimed at eliciting laughter (R. Lebègue, "Rabelais devant l'écolier limousin," *Mercure de France*, CCCIV [October, 1948], 275).

7. The groundwork for the study of the Library of Saint Victor was done by Paul Lacroix, *Catalogue de la bibliothèque de Saint Victor* (Paris, 1861). A. H. Schutz thinks that Rabelais includes this chapter to cast a blow at the abbey which had aligned itself with the Sorbonne against the new Humanism ("Why did Rabelais satirize the Library of Saint Victor," *Modern Language Notes* [January], 1953, 39–41).

8. Rabelais derives this cock and bull verbiage, "coq-à-l'âne" or

"fatrasie" in French, from medieval theater. Marot, Rabelais's contemporary, made this genre quite fashionable in his time; cf. R. Garapon, *La Fantaisie verbale et le comique dans le théâtre français du moyen âge à la fin du XVIIe siècle* (Paris, 1957), and H. Meylan, *Epitres du coq-à-l'âne: Contribution à l'histoire de la satire au XVIe siècle* (Geneva, 1956).

9. Much has been written about Rabelais's debt to Folengo and Pulci; this criticism resembles a tug-of-war; the French pull him toward them and tend to minimize the importance of the Italian influence, and the Italian magnify it, often to the point of distortion: Lazar Sainéan, "Les Sources modernes du roman de Rabelais," *Revue des Etudes Rabelaisiennes*, X (1912), 375–420; Cordelia del Fiume, *De l'influence de quelques auteurs italiens sur François Rabelais* (Florence, 1918); Pietro Toldo, "L'Arte italiana nell'opera di Francesco Rabelais," *Archiv für das Studium der Neueren Sprachen und Literaturen* (1898), 103–45; Giovanni Tancredi, "Il Margutte del Pulci, il Cingar del Folengo e il Panurgo del Rabelais," *Atti del Congresso Internazionale di Scienze Storiche*, V (1904), pp. 227–39; Benjamin Bart, "Aspects of the Comic in Pulci and Rabelais," *Modern Language Quarterly*, XI (June, 1950), 156–63.

10. For an explanation of the linguistic origins of concocted languages see E. Pons, "Les Langues imaginaires dans le voyage. Les Jargons de Panurge dans Rabelais," *Revue de Litterature Comparée*, IX (1931), 185–218.

11. A detailed list of Panurge's tricks can be found in Jean Plattard, *L'Oeuvre de Rabelais: sources, inventions et compositions* (Paris, 1910), pp. 323–26; Paul Stapfer, *Rabelais, sa personne, son génie, son oeuvre* (Paris, 1889), pp. 284–88; Pierre Villey, *Rabelais et Marot* (Paris, 1923), pp. 175–76.

12. Jean Lessellier, "Deux enfants naturels de Rabelais légitimés par le pape Paul III," *Humanisme et Renaissance*, V (1938), 548–70. Supposedly Rabelais had three children; in addition to the one who died, the two in question in this article were by another woman and were never heard of.

13. Leo Spitzer sees an abysmal quality in Rabelais's giganticism which would recall Hugo's "bouche d'ombre" ("Le prétendu réalisme de Rabelais," *Modern Philology*, XXXVII [1939–40], 139–50). In fact, the irreality of the universe inside of Pantagruel assumes a frightening super-reality. The playful element ought not, however, be disregarded.

Notes and References

Chapter Two

1. For the relationship between Rabelais and Saint-Gelais see Jean Plattard, "Rabelais et Mellin de Saint-Gelais," *Revue des Etudes Rabelaisiennes,* IX (1911), 106–08; cf. my *Etude . . .* pp. 7–8. Lately the second engima has been deciphered as a paraphrase of some of St. Paul's epistles in which the apostle warns his disciple Timothy against those who would pervert Christ's doctrine; cf. E. Telle, "Thélème et le Paulinisme matrimonial erasmien: le sens de l'énigme en prophétie," *François Rabelais. Ouvrage publié pour le quatrième centenaire de sa mort (1553–1953)* (Geneva, 1953), pp. 114–18. Along a different line of criticism see R. L. Frautschi, "The 'Enigme en Prophétie' and the question of authorship," *French Studies,* XVII (1963), 331–39.

2. Marcel Françon, *Les Croniques admirables du puissant roy Gargantua* (Rochecorbon, Indre-et-Loire, 1956), pp. xliii–xlvii.

3. Paul Sebillot, *Gargantua dans les traditions populaires* (Paris, 1883); Henri Dontenville, *La Mythologie française* (Paris, 1948).

4. Introduction to Lefranc's edition of *Pantagruel,* pp. li–lii; and M. A. Screech, *L'Evangélisme de Rabelais,* (Geneva, 1959), pp. 10–19.

5. A complete study of Rabelais's use of proverbs is still lacking. L. Sainéan only catalogues proverbs in *La Langue de Rabelais,* I (Paris, 1922), pp. 342–448. A step in the right direction was taken by Eleanor O'Kane, "The Proverb: Rabelais and Cervantes," *Comparative Literature,* II (1950), 360–69; and I continue to show the esthetic use of proverbs in my *Etude . . . ,* pp. 96–97.

6. Villey, *Rabelais,* p. 401; B. Ravà, *L'Art de Rabelais* (Rome, 1910), p. 118.

7. François Rabelais, *Gargantua,* ed. Abel Lefranc (Paris, 1912), pp. liv–lxxii.

8. This episode is one of the most obvious ones used to substantiate Rabelais's Paulinism and the infiltration of the Reform in his works.

9. Critics have tried to establish the origin or the prototype in real life of Friar John, but without much success. Georges Lote thinks that Rabelais has drawn a self-portrait (*La Vie et l'oeuvre de François Rabelais* [Paris, 1938], p. 362). Plattard, on the contrary, sees this character as an original creation on Rabelais's part (*Rabelais* [1910], p. 24). Lefranc in the introduction to *Gargantua* (p. lxxix) believes that Rabelais models Friar John on an abbot from the Abbey of Seuillé, the very abbey that the monk is defending.

10. If one wishes, the episode can be transposed to a historical plane contemporaneous with Rabelais's times; then Gargantua becomes

François I, and Picrochole, Charles V. Such a slant, of course, fits in very well with the dated, though still valid, view of Rabelais as a propagandist for his king.

11. "Pyrrhus," *Plutarch's Lives*, trans. Bernadotte Perrin (New York, 1920), pp. 387–89.

12. Michel de Montaigne, "De l'inégalité qui est entre nous," *Essais*, ed. M. Rat (Paris, 1962), p. 259; N. Boileau-Despréaux, *Epistres*, ed. A. Cahen (Paris, 1936), first epistle; Jean de La Fontaine in "Perrette et le pot au lait" (Perrette and the milk jug).

13. Scholarship on the Abbey of Thélème abounds, of course; it stresses the meaning which the episode supposedly has and the interpretations vary with the critics, as a skeletal sample shows: evangelical (Lefranc in introduction, pp. l–lvi, mostly because each Thélèmite has his own chapel and does not go to community services; Febvre readily rejects this view [*Le Problème de l'incroyance*, p. 112]), praising free will and Christian liberty (Screech, *Evangélisme*, p. 37, and *The Rabelaisian Marriage* [London, 1958], pp. 27–36); hedonistic (S. Eskin, "Mythic Unity in Rabelais," *PMLA*, LXXIX [1964], 552). Some common sense is injected into the matter by A. J. Krailsheimer, *Rabelais and the Franciscans* (London, 1963), pp. 156–158; according to this critic too much meaning and originality is being read into the episode. The answer may lie with F. Desonay who stresses the gratuitous aspects instead of the ideological meaning of the tale ("En relisant l'Abbaye de Thélème," *Ouvrage pour le quatrième centenaire*, pp. 93–103).

Chapter Three

1. During the sixteenth century one finds a continuation of the ambivalent medieval attitude toward women. In the Middle Ages the *fabliaux* illustrated the harsh downgrading opinion toward women while the romances idealized woman. During the Renaissance, the ideological and literary struggle continues. The Platonic argument of idealization finds a supporter, among others, in H. Heroët's *Parfaicte Amye* (1542) ("The Ideal Lady"), and the opposite current produces, with ironic undertones in the titles, T. Sebillet's *Louenge des Femmes* ("In Praise of Women") and B. de la Borderie's *L'Amye de court*. For a detailed account of the Quarrel, see the introduction to the critical edition of the *Third Book* by Lefranc (Paris, 1931), pp. xliv–lv; or E. Telle, *L'Oeuvre de Marguerite d'Angoulême, reine de Navarre et la Querelle des Femmes* (Toulouse, 1937).

2. The praise of debts has been considered a satire of Marsilio Ficino, a fifteenth-century Platonist philosopher, according to whom love is the moving force of the universe. Rabelais then would substitute

Notes and References

whimsically debts for love; see R. Marichal, "L'Attitude de Rabelais devant le néoplatonisme et l'italianisme," *Ouvrage publié pour le IVe centenaire de sa mort*, p. 186.

3. C. A. Mayer, "Rabelais's Satirical Eulogy: the Praise of Borrowing," *ibid.*, pp. 147–55.

4. See my *Etude* . . . , pp. 31–32.

5. The most comprehensive and synthesizing study has been done by V.-L. Saulnier, "L'Enigme du Pantagruélion," *Études Rabelaisiennes*, I (1956), 51–56.

6. A. Thibaudet, "Rabelais, le tonneau et la table," *Nouvelles Littéraires*, X (August 29, 1931), 1.

7. Molière will use the same technique in his *Mariage forcé* in a dialogue between Sganarelle, one of Panurge's literary offsprings, and Parphurius, a Pyrrhonic philosopher.

8. Considerable scholarship has covered the Bridoye (Bridlegoose) episode. M. A. Screech has used it to show further the Pauline influence on Rabelais as well as the importance of the will of God in human decision (*The Rabelaisian Marriage*, pp. 116 *et seq.*). In a painstaking task, J. D. M. Derrett has identified, whenever possible, the sources of Bridlegoose's abundant allegations ("Rabelais's Legal Learning and the Trial of Bridoye," *Bibliothèque* d'Humanisme et Renaissance, XXV [1963], pp. 111–71). M. A. Screech has continued this work, and may be on a safer track this time, as he deals with the esthetic aspects of the episode and declares that the humor of the episode "lies above all in Bridoye's abuse of commonplaces" ("The Legal Comedy of Rabelais in the Trial of Bridoye in the *Tiers Livre de Pantagruel*," *Études Rabelaissiennes*, V [1964], pp. 175–95; cf. Enzo Nardi, *Rabelais e il diritto romano* (Milan: Giuffrè, 1962), pp. 131–218.

9. Screech, *The Rabelaisian Marriage*, pp. 105 *et seq.*

10. For an example of this device see E. Droz, *Le Recueil de Trepperel*, I (Paris, 1935), p. 32; or my *Etude*, p. 102. Because Rabelais enumerates in columns, one becomes more aware of the relationship of meanings and sounds, whereas the medieval playwrights wrote in verse form. A. Luzio claims that Rabelais derived the idea from Folengo (*Studi Folenghiani* [Florence, 1897], p. 23).

11. Finally in a recent work, an attempt has been made to analyze Rabelais as a story teller; see A. Keller, *The Telling of Tales in Rabelais—Aspects of his Narrative Art* (Frankfurt am Main, 1963). The first two chapters deal specifically, but not exhaustively, with techniques of narrative and fill an important gap in Rabelais scholarship.

12. Plattard, *Rabelais* (1910), pp. 331–32.

13. This last tale has attracted much attention; see Pietro Toldo.

"La Fumée du rôti et la divination des signes," *Revue des Etudes Rabelaisiennes*, I (1903), 13–14; Ernest Langlois, "La Fumée du rôti payé au son de l'argent," *Revue des Etudes Rabelaisiennes*, I (1903), 222–24; and L. Sozzi, "Rabelais, Philelphe et le 'fumet du rôti'," *Etudes Rabelaisiennes*, V (1964), 197–205. All these try to give sources for the tale, and in the last article the author even gets angry because Rabelais did not follow closely his model. Of what use then is Rabelais's own creative imagination?

14. Lefranc, Introduction to the *Third Book*, p. lv.

15. M. A. Screech, "An Interpretation of the Querelle des Amyes," *Bibliothèque d'Humanisme et Renaissance*, XXI (1959), 125.

16. V.-L. Saulnier, *Le Dessein de Rabelais* (Paris, 1957), pp. 51–62.

17. Walter Kaiser, "Rabelais's Panurge" in *Praisers of Folly* (Cambridge, Mass., 1963), pp. 103–92; the same Pauline interpretation is, of course, stressed in M. A. Screech's *The Rabelaisian Marriage*.

Chapter Four

1. Abel Lefranc has tried to show the actual route that Pantagruel took by asserting that Rabelais gives imaginary names to real places, a questionable task, in *Les Navigations de Pantagruel* (Paris, 1905).

2. For the relationship between Rabelais and Calcagnini see *Arthur Tilley*, Rabelais (Philadelphia, 1907), p. 231; and S. Eskin, "Physis and Antiphysie: The Idea of Nature in Rabelais and Calcagnini," *Comparative Literature*, XIV (1962), 167–73.

3. Georges Lote (*Rabelais*, pp. 129–30) places the episode of Lent in a proper perspective by tracing it to its medieval sources. Recently, following the Lefranc school of criticism, the episodes of Lent and the Chitterlings have been put in a distorted historical context; each kind of Chitterling is identified with a specific Protestant sect (Alban Krailsheimer, "The Andouilles of the *Quart Livre*," *Ouvrage publié pour le quatrième centenaire de sa mort*, pp. 226–32). At this point it may be proper to suggest that the usual translation of *andouilles* as "Chitterling" is quite misleading; the work means actually "link sausage," and thusly translated it would then make more sense in the action and carry the amorphic suggestions of the episode when they are compared to man.

4. Every general study on Rabelais touches on this subject; among many see Bonaventura Zumbini, "Gli episodi dei montoni e della tempesta presso il Folengo e presso il Rabelais," *Nozze Percopo-Luciani: 30 luglio 1902* (Naples, 1903), pp. 175–83; cf. also Chapter 1, note 9. For a new approach to Folengo and Rabelais see my own "Rabelais and Folengo," *Comparative Literature*, XV (Fall, 1963), 357–64.

Notes and References

5. R. Marichal, "*Quart Livre*, Commentaires," *Etudes Rabelais-iennes*, I (1956), 171–78.

6. R. Marichal, "*Quart Livre*, Commentaires," pp. 183 and 186. Although excellent, this article continues to give the historical critical approach to the Gaster Episode (pp. 183–202), but the esthetic approach is left out. The author, for example, finds still another influence on Rabelais's Gaster, Jean Lemaire de Belges's *Concorde des deux Langages*.

7. Rabelais leaves no doubt in the reader's mind about the allusion to Virgil: "Do you remember Aeneas, caught in a storm near Sicily, regretting that he had not perished at the hands of valiant Diomedes, the Grecian hero? Thrice-blessed, four times happy, he said are those who gave up the ghost in the Trojan fires" (IV, 22).

8. If she saves him from the storm, Cingar promises to offer the Virgin Mary a candle as big as a mast. Once the danger is passed, he conveniently forgets about it.

9. For detailed studies of the nautical vocabulary in Rabelais, see Lazar Sainéan, *La Langue de Rabelais*, I, pp. 99–125; Robert Marichal, "Le Nom des vents chez Rabelais," *Etudes Rabelaisiennes*, I (1956), 7–28; L. Denoix, "Les Connaissances nautiques de Rabelais," *Ouvrage publié pour le quatrième centenaire*, pp. 171–80.

10. Some try to find a source in real life for Basché; cf. R. Marichal, "René Du Puy et les Chicanous," *Bibliothèque d'Humanisme et Renaissance*, IX (1949), 136 *et seq.*

11. Screech, *L'Evangélisme de Rabelais*, pp. 77–83.

12. A. Le Double, *Rabelais, anatomiste et physiologiste* (Paris, 1899), p. 411.

13. For an interpretation of this episode as an aspect of Rabelais's hesuchism, a non-predicatory evangelism, see V.-L. Saulnier, "Le Silence de Rabelais et le mythe des paroles gelées," *Ouvrage pour le quatrième Centenaire*, pp. 233–47. A more literary interpretation is given by Jean Guiton, "Le Mythe des paroles gelées," *Romanic Review*, XXXI (1940), 3–15.

Chapter Five

1. Villey, *Rabelais*, p. 320. The prologues have recently attracted renewed attention; cf. Floyd Gray, "Structure and Meaning in the Prologue to the *Tiers Livre*," *L'Esprit Créateur* III (Summer, 1963), 57–62, and "Ambiguity and Point of view in the Prologue to *Gargantua*," *Romanic Review*, LVI (February, 1965), 12–21.

2. See Lefranc's Introduction to the *Third Book*, pp. xx–xxviii. Lote, *Rabelais*, pp. 261–322.

3. Pierre de la Juillière, *Les Images de Rabelais* (Halle, a.S., 1912), p. 7. The translation is my own.

4. For an interpretation of this episode as an indication of Rabelais's belief in predestination, see Screech, *L'Evangélisme de Rabelais*, p. 66.

5. A detailed study, though often peripheral, of the role of music in Rabelais has been made by Nan Cooke Carpenter, *Rabelais and Music* (Chapel Hill, N.C., 1954).

6. Jean Rousset, *La Littérature de l'âge baroque en France* (Paris, 1954), pp. 14 and 90; for an interpretation of Rabelais seen in a baroque light see my own "Rabelais: a Precursor of the Baroque Style," *Rivista di Letteratura Moderne e Comparate*, XVII (March, 1964), 5–16.

Chapter Six

1. Because the question of education in Rabelais, though still significant, may be somewhat antiquated at present, we have taken it as a point of departure for an analysis of his style, thus rejuvenating the topic and replacing it in the work in an enlightening perspective. In addition to the specific chapters devoted to education in general studies on Rabelais, see also: Albert Coutaud, *La Pédagogie de Rabelais* (Paris, 1899); V.-L. Saulnier, Les Idées pédagogiques de Rabelais," *Bulletin des Amis de Rabelais et de la Devinière*, I (1961), 279–81; F. Stoppoloni, *Rabelais e il suo pensiero educativo* (Rome, 1906); G. Giraldi, *Rabelais e l'educazione del principe* (Milan, 1953).

2. For a rich summary of the criticism which this letter has elicited, see M. Françon, *Autour de la lettre de Gargantua à son fils* (Rochecorbon, Indre-et-Loire, 1957).

3. A recent study, emphasizing several abortive renaissances prior to the sixteenth century, has shown the various Italian roots of the French Renaissance; cf. Franco Simone, *Il Rinascimento francese* (Turin, 1961).

4. Among others, Alain has placed into a meaningful perspective the constant presence of huge amounts of food, especially in the first two books. According to him, and rightly so, this element has a harmless effect, morally speaking; cf. *Propos* (Paris, 1956), pp. 313–14.

5. Stapfer gives a detailed account of a day's activities at Montaigu (*Rabelais*, pp. 296–97).

6. C.-A. Sainte-Beuve, "Rabelais," *Les Grands écrivains français*, ed. Maurice Allem, III (Paris, 1926), p. 33. The translation is my own.

7. Lote, *Rabelais*, pp. 194–95.

8. Among the many studies devoted to this comparison, see for example: Eugène Réaume, *Rabelais et Montaigne pédagogue* (Paris,

1886); P. Hoffman, *Italienische Humanisten und Rabelais und Montaigne als Pädogogen* (Stettin, 1876).

Chapter Seven

1. Sainte-Beuve, "Rabelais," pp. 39–40.

2. For a detailed analysis of these elements, see Lefranc's Introduction to *Pantagruel*, pp. xl–li.

3. Jean Plattard, "L'Ecriture Sainte dans l'oeuvre de Rabelais," *Revue des Etudes Rabelaisiennes*, VIII (1910), 293–94; E. Gilson "Rabelais franciscain," *Les Idées et les lettres* (Paris, 1932), p. 218; L. Febvre, *Le Problème de l'incroyance au XVIe siècle*, p. 180; Jacques Boulenger, *Rabelais* (Paris, 1942), p. 169; and lately Enrico Bertalot, "Rabelais et la Bible d'après les quatre premiers livres," *Etudes Rabelaisiennes*, V (1964), p. 20.

4. In *Quelques aspects de la pensée de Rabelais* (Paris, 1954), Paulette Lenoir follows Lefranc's footsteps. Henri Busson, ("Rabelais et le miracle," *Le Rationalisme dans la littérature de la Renaissance* [Paris, 1957], pp. 157–68) modifies slightly his earlier position. In the first edition of his book (1922), he blindly followed Lefranc, but now he states that it is difficult to know when Rabelais plays or is serious. J. R. Charbonnel considers Rabelais a free thinker in *La Pensée Italienne au XVIe siècle et le courant libertin* (Paris, 1917), pp. 716–17.

5. In *Le Problème de l'incroyance en France*, Febvre did the most to rehabilitate Rabelais along this line of interpretation.

6. Gilson, "Rabelais franciscain," pp. 231–35.

7. H. Jacoubet, "L'Enigme de Rabelais," *Variétés d'histoire littéraire* (Paris, 1935), pp. 11–31.

8. Cf. Febvre, *Le Problème de l'incroyance*, pp. 226–56.

9. Introduction to *Gargantua*, p. xxvi.

10. Screech, *L'Evangélisme de Rabelais*, pp. 10–19.

11. *Ibid.*, pp. 23–37.

12. *Ibid.*, p. 66.

13. The latest confirmation of this position is made by A. J. Krailsheimer, *Rabelais and the Franciscans* (Oxford, 1963): "Rabelais was a Christian at all times, and that being so, held the truth of the Christian revelation to be absolute in the face of any rational attack" (p. 217).

14. A thorough study of Rabelais in the sixteenth century has been made by Marcel de Grève, *L'interprétation de Rabelais au XVIe siècle* (Geneva, 1961); cf. L. Sainéan, *L'Influence et la réputation de Rabelais* (Paris, 1930); Jacques Boulenger, *Rabelais à travers les âges* (Paris, 1925).

15. For a study of stoicism in Rabelais's thought, see M. A. Screech, "Some Stoic Elements in Rabelais's religious thought (the Will-Destiny-Active Virtue)," *Etudes Rabelaisiennes,* I (1956), pp. 73–97.

16. A systematic study of Platonism in Rabelais's works is still lacking, perhaps because of the dubious validity of such a global approach; for partial attempts see: R. Marichal, "L'Attitude de Rabelais devant le néoplatonisme," *Ouvrage publié pour le quatrième centenaire,* pp. 181–209; L. Febvre, *Le Problème de l'incroyance,* pp. 287, 307, 409; J. Plattard, *Rabelais* (1910), pp. 221–25; A. Lefranc, "Le Platon de Rabelais," *Bulletin du Bibliophile* (1901), pp. 105–14, 169–81.

Selected Bibliography

I SPECIALIZED BIBLIOGRAPHIES

Cabeen, David C., ed. *A Critical Bibliography of French Literature. The Sixteenth Century.* Syracuse: Syracuse University Press, 1956, nn. 817–916.

Cioranescu, Alexandre. *Bibliographie de la littérature française au 16e siècle.* Paris: Librairie C. Klincksieck, 1959, nn. 17933–18789.

Cordié, Carlo. "Recenti studi sulla vita e sulle opere di François Rabelais, 1939–1950," *Letterature Moderne,* I (1950), 107–20.

Plan, Pierre-Paul. *Bibliographie rabelaisienne: Les éditions de Rabelais de 1532 à 1711.* Paris: Imprimerie Nationale, 1904.

Plattard, Jean. *Etat présent des études rabelaisiennes.* Paris: Société d'édition "Les belles lettres," 1927.

Rackow, Paul. "Der gegenwärtige Stand der Rabelais-Forschung," *Germanisch-romanische Monatschrift,* XVIII (1930), 198–211 and 277–90. Rabelais studies up to 1930.

Saulnier, Verdun-Louis. "Dix années d'études rabelaisiennes," *Bibliothèque d'Humanisme et Renaissance,* XI (1949), 104–28. Rabelais studies from 1939–49; covers the same period of time as Cordié's article.

Schrader, Ludvig. "Die Rabelais-Forschung der Jahre 1950–1960: Tendenzen und Ergebnisse," *Romanistisches Jahrbuch,* XI (1960), 161–201. Rabelais studies for the indicated decade.

II IMPORTANT EDITIONS OF RABELAIS'S WORKS

Oeuvres, Edition Varorium. 9 vols. Paris: Dalibon, 1823–26. Noteworthy for its critical comments by scholars up to that time.

Oeuvres, ed. Charles Marty-Laveaux. 6 vols. Paris: Lemerre, 1868–1903. The standard edition of the nineteenth century.

Oeuvres, ed. Abel Lefranc and Robert Marichal *et al.* 7 vols. Paris and Geneva: E. Champion and E. Droz, 1912–65. A basic tool for Rabelais studies, a model critical edition. The first three books were published under the editorship of Abel Lefranc (1912–31)

and the *Fourth Book* under Robert Marichal (1955 and 1966).
[to be published]

Oeuvres complètes, ed. Jean Plattard. 5 vols. Paris: F. Roches, 1929.
A standard, though dated work, which is based on the above critical edition.

Pantagruel, ed. Verdun-Louis Saulnier. Geneva: Droz, 1946. This edition profits from scholarship done since the critical edition.

Le Quart Livre, ed. Robert Marichal. Geneva: Droz, 1947. A needed
work at the time but now superseded by the recent critical edition.

L'Abbaye de Thélème, ed. Raoul Morçay. Geneva: Droz, 1947. More
important for its introduction than the text.

Oeuvres complètes, ed. Marcel Guilbaud. 5 vols. Paris: Imprimerie nationale, 1957. The standard edition in modernized French.

Oeuvres complètes, ed. Jacques Boulenger and Lucien Scheler (Bibliothèque de la Pléiade). Paris: Gallimard, 1959. A standard and
compact edition with a very adequate critical apparatus.

Oeuvres complètes, ed. Pierre Jourda. 2 vols. Paris: Garnier, 1962. A
standard edition equal to the one in the above Pléiade collection.

Le Tiers Livre, ed. M. A. Screech. Geneva: Droz, 1964. A timely
work which takes into account scholarship since the last critical
edition.

III STANDARD TRANSLATIONS

François Rabelais. *Gargantua and Pantagruel,* trans. Sir Thomas Urquhart and Peter Le Motteaux. Chicago: Encyclopedia Britannica,
1955. The first translation of Rabelais's works into English. Urquhart translated the first two books in 1653 and the *Third Book* in
1693. Le Motteux translated the *Fourth Book* and the *Fifth Book*
in 1694. See the Preface.

François Rabelais. *Gargantua and Pantagruel,* trans. Jacques Le Clercq
(The Modern Library). New York: Random House, 1936.

François Rabelais. *Gargantua and Pantagruel,* trans. John Michael
Cohen. Baltimore: Penguin Books, 1955.

François Rabelais. *Gargantua and Pantagruel: Selections,* trans. Floyd
Gray. New York: Appleton-Century-Crofts, 1966.

IV IMPORTANT PERIODICALS

Revue des Etudes Rabelaisiennes (1903–12). This journal, though no
longer solely devoted to Rabelais but to the Renaissance as a
whole, continued under the following titles: *Revue du Seizième
Siècle* (1913–32), *Humanisme et Renaissance* (1934–40), and
Bibliothèque d'Humanisme et Renaissance (1941 to present).

Selected Bibliography

Bulletin de l'Association des Amis de Rabelais et de la Devinière (1951 to present).

Etudes Rabelaisiennes (1959 to present). A yearly publication in which some volumes appear as books.

V COMMEMORATIVE PUBLICATIONS FOR RABELAIS'S QUADRICENTENNIAL

François Rabelais. Ouvrage publié pour le quatrième centenaire de sa mort. Geneva: Droz, 1953.

Carrefour (February 11, 1953).

Les Nouvelles Littéraires (April 9, 1953).

L'Education Nationale (April 16, 1953).

Europe (November–December 1953).

Samuel F. Will. "The Rabelais Quadricentennial, 1953," *French Review,* XXVIII (January, 1955), 233–40.

VI IMPORTANT CRITICAL STUDIES

Auerbach, Eric. "The World in Pantagruel's Mouth," *Mimesis,* trans. Warland R. Trask. Princeton: Princeton University Press, 1953, pp. 262–84. A very perceptive look into Rabelais's conception of reality.

Besant, Walter. *Rabelais.* Philadelphia: Lippincott, 1879. A very antiquated study that indicated a short-sighted attitude in the English-speaking world.

Boulenger, Jacques. *Rabelais.* Paris: Editions Colbert, 1942. A good introduction to Rabelais, though a little heavy on the biographical side.

Brown, Huntington. *Rabelais in English Literature.* Cambridge (Mass.): Harvard University Press, 1933. Competent and needed study but emphasis on post seventeenth-century literature.

Busson, Henri. *Le Rationalisme dans la littérature française de la Renaissance.* Paris: Vrin, 1957, pp. 157–68. A basic study on the subject of free-thinking writers in which the position toward Rabelais is ambiguous (and rightly so).

Carpenter, Nan Cooke. *Rabelais and Music.* Chapel Hill (North Carolina): The University of North Carolina Press, 1954. The only book on the subject; the treatment of the subject is often peripheral and tenuous.

Chappell, Arthur F. *The Enigma of Rabelais: An Essay in Interpretation.* Cambridge: The University Press, 1924. For its time a solid and sensible interpretation of Rabelais, but with no serious reference to style.

Charpentier, John. *Rabelais et le génie de la Renaissance*. Paris: Tallandier, 1946. Sees a comic didacticism in the books.

Dieguez, Manuel de. *Rabelais par lui-même*. Paris: Editions du Seuil, 1960. An excellent little study which emphasizes the evolution of Rabelais's language.

Dontenville, Henri. *La Mythologie française*. Paris: Payot, 1948. The best work available tracing the legend of Gargantua in popular tradition.

Faguet, Emile. *Le Seizième siècle; études littéraires*. Paris: Société française d'imprimerie et de librairie, 1902. In spite of its date contains some very pertinent and keen observations.

Febvre, Lucien. *Le Problème de l'incroyance au XVIe siècle, la religion de Rabelais*. Paris: A. Michel, 1942. An indispensable book for the rehabilitation of Rabelais's thought.

France, Anatole. *Rabelais*. Paris: Calmann-Lévy, 1928. Translated by Ernest Boyd, New York: H. Holt, 1929. Of interest because it shows an affinity of mind between the two writers.

Françon, Marcel, ed. *Les Croniques admirables du puissant roy Gargantua*. Rochecorbon (Indre-et-Loire): C. Gay, 1956. The latest edition of one of the "Gargantuine" chronicles.

―――. *Autour de la lettre de Gargantua à son fils*. Rochecorbon (Indre-et-Loire): C. Gay, 1957. Contains a good summary of criticism on the subject.

Frye, Northrop. *Anatomy of Criticism*. Princeton (N.J.): Princeton University Press, 1957, pp. 232–36, 308–13. Pungent pages on satire and structure.

Gebhart, Emile. *Rabelais, la Réforme et la Renaissance*. Paris: Hachette, 1904. Points out medieval aspects of Rabelais then puts him in a reasonable light, but the Lefranc storm was soon to drown out this study.

Glauser, Alfred. *Rabelais Créateur*. Paris: Nizet, 1966. A much-needed addition to scholarship on Rabelais who is viewed here as a literary artist.

Grève, Marcel de. *L'Interprétation de Rabelais au XVIe siècle*. Geneva: Droz, 1961. A very thorough treatment of the subject which also gives an idea of literary criticism in the sixteenth century.

Hatzfeld, Helmut. *François Rabelais*. Munich: G. Paetel, 1923. A sensitive approach to Rabelais which has not gained proper recognition because it is written in German.

Huguet, Edmond E. *Etude sur la syntaxe de Rabelais, comparée à celle des autres prosateurs de 1450 à 1550*. Paris: Hachette, 1894. An essential but quite dated study on the subject.

Jourda, Pierre. *Le Gargantua de Rabelais*. Paris: SFELT, 1948. Contains some of the best comments on *Gargantua* with some feeling for the style.

Juillière, Pierre de la. *Les Images de Rabelais*. Halle: N. Niemeyer, 1912. A catalogue of the imagery in Rabelais but with no esthetic approach.

Kaiser, Walter, "Rabelais's Panurge," *Praisers of Folly*. Cambridge (Mass.): Harvard University Press, 1963. pp. 101–92. An imaginative re-evaluation of the *Third Book* along evangelistic and philosophical lines.

Keller, Abraham. *The Telling of Tales in Rabelais—Aspects of His Narrative Art*. Frankfurt am Main: V. Klostermann, 1963. A much-needed study, though incomplete; quite valuable within its self-limited scope.

Kline, Michael. *Rabelais and the Age of Printing*. Geneva: Droz, 1963. Very peripheral in its approach, title even misleading.

Kraislheimer, Alban J. *Rabelais and the Franciscans*. Oxford: Clarendon Press, 1963. A fresh and sensible approach to many questions facing Rabelais scholarship.

Lebègue, Raymond. *Rabelais*. Tübingen: N. Niemeyer, 1952. A general but up-to-date monograph.

Lecuyer, Maurice. *Balzac et Rabelais*. Paris: Société d'édition "Les belles lettres," 1956. Based more on what has been done on the subject than what ought to be done.

Lefebvre, Henri. *Rabelais*. Paris: Editeurs français réunis, 1955. Perceptive at times but loses from its Marxist approach.

Lewis, Wyndham. *Doctor Rabelais*. London: Sheed and Ward, 1957. A stimulating appraisal that takes account of the artistic merits of Rabelais's works.

Lote, Georges. *La Vie et l'oeuvre de François Rabelais*. Paris: Droz, 1938. The best introductory work available; both content and style receive ample treatment.

Plattard, Jean. *L'Invention et la composition dans l'oeuvre de Rabelais*. Paris: Champion, 1910. A basic tool to any specialized approach to Rabelais.

———. *La Vie de François Rabelais*. Paris and Brussels: Van Oest, 1928. Translated by Louis P. Roche as *The Life of François Rabelais*. Alfred A. Knopf, 1931. The standard biography.

Poirier, Adolphe. *La Langue de Rabelais. Les Influences du Bas-Poitou*. Paris: Editions D'Artey, 1944. A cataloguing of words from Rabelais's native region.

Powys, John C. *Rabelais, his Life*. London: Bodley Head, 1948. Leans heavily on French scholarship; interesting confrontation with Shakespeare.

Putnam, Samuel. *François Rabelais. Man of the Renaissance, a Spiritual Biography*. New York, J. Cape and H. Smith, 1930. Used to be a standard introduction to Rabelais, to be used with caution.

Sainéan, Lazare. *L'Histoire naturelle et les branches connexes dans l'oeuvre de Rabelais*. Paris: Champion, 1921. The only study on the natural sciences in Rabelais's books.

———. *La Langue de Rabelais*. 2 vols. Paris: E. de Boccard, 1921. A fundamental work on the language; includes imagery, proverbs, sources of words, unfortunately in catalogue form.

———. "Le Cinquième livre de Rabelais," *Problèmes littéraires du seizième siècle*. Paris: E. de Boccard, 1927, pp. 1–98. Believes that the *Fifth Book* is mostly authentic.

———. *L'Influence et la réputation de Rabelais*. Paris: J. Gamber, 1930. Opinions on and influences of Rabelais in France and abroad; complements Jacques Boulenger's *Rabelais à travers les âges*. Paris: Le Divan, 1925.

Sainte-Beuve, Charles-Augustin. "Rabelais," *Les Grands Ecrivains français*, ed. Maurice Allem. III, Paris: Garnier, 1926, pp. 23–41. Some of the best pages written on Rabelais.

Saulnier, Verdun-Louis. *Le Dessein de Rabelais*. Paris: Société d'édition d'enseignement supérieur, 1957. Especially important for its new approach to the *Third Book* along quest-for-happiness lines.

Screech, Michael A. *The Rabelaisian Marriage, Aspects of Rabelais's Religion, Ethics and Comic Philosophy*. London: E. Arnold, 1958. Emphasis on Paulinism in Rabelais; comic elements quite muddled.

———. *L'Evangélisme de Rabelais*. Geneva: Droz, 1959. Rabelais put in Protestant camp up to a certain point, sometimes small amount of text is given too much weight.

Sébillot, Paul. *Gargantua dans les traditions populaires*. Complements the Dontenville book but also superseded by it.

Spitzer, Leo. *Die Wortbildung als stilistisches Mittel exemplifiert an Rabelais*. Halle: N. Niemeyer, 1910. A fundamental work that launches stylistic studies on Rabelais.

———. "Rabelais et les 'rabelaisants,' " *Studi Francesi*, IV (September–December 1960), 401–23. Takes issue with the Abel Lefranc school of criticism and advocates a more esthetic approach.

Stapfer, Paul. *Rabelais, sa personne, son génie, son oeuvre*. Paris: Colin, 1889. An introduction to Rabelais too often neglected but that contains some fine critical appreciation.

Telle, Emile. *L'Oeuvre de Marguerite d'Angoulême, reine de Navarre, et la Querelle des Femmes*. Toulouse: Imprimerie toulousaine Lion et fils, 1937. Important for its discussion of the Quarrel of Women in the Renaissance.

Tetel, Marcel. *Etude sur le comique de Rabelais*. Florence: L. Olschki, 1964. A study on the comic mostly from the stylistic point of view.

Thuasne, Louis. *Études sur Rabelais*. Paris, E. Bouillon, 1904. Shows some influences on Rabelais, sometimes most tenuous.

Tilley, Arthur A. *François Rabelais*. Philadelphia and London: J. B. Lippincott, 1907. Biographical part is dated; interesting questions on the *Third Book*.

————. "Rabelais and the Fifth Book," *Studies in French Renaissance*. Cambridge: The University Press, 1922, pp. 85–122. Believes work is by Rabelais but with some later interpolations by editors.

Villey, Pierre. *Rabelais et Marot*. Paris: E. Champion, 1923. Sees the comic as a vehicle for ideas and emphasizes the learned aspects of the books.

Weinberg, Bernard. "Rabelais as an Artist," *Texas Quarterly*, III (1960), 175–88. A succinct and valuable contribution to the subject.

Willcocks, Mary P. *The Laughing Philosopher, Being a Life of François Rabelais*. London: Allen and Unwin, 1950. Some acute remarks on Rabelais's thought along moderating lines but no real contributions on the "laughing philosopher."

Index

Molière, 26

Montaigne, 45, 91, 96, 112; "Of Children's Education," 112–13; "The Cannibals," 114

Montpellier, University of, 17

More, Sir Thomas, 21, 25, 112; *Utopia,* 21

Nasuerm, Alcofribas (pseudonym of Rabelais), 49

Orlando Furioso, 82

Pantagruelism, 123–24

Pausanias, 102; *Monuments,* 102

Plato, 51, 102; *Banquet,* 51; *Dialogues,* 102

Pliny, 51, 60; *Natural History,* 60

Plutarch, 44, 80, 88, 92; *Morals,* 102; *Symposiacs,* 92

Politian, 88

Ponticus, Heraclides, 88

Ptolemy, 91

Pulci, Luigi, 18; *Il Morgante,* 18, 19, 26

Pyrrhus, 23, 44

Querelle des Femmes, 49

Rabelais, Antoine (father), 38

Rabelais, approach to learning, 100; humanism, 100–104; views on medieval education, 104–108; belief in physical exercise, 109–110; his coining of words, 110–111; views on ethics and morals, 113–116; contrasting interpretations of, 117–26

WRITINGS OF:

Fourth Book, The, 60, 65–81; theme and structure, 65–71; verbal invention in, 66–67; sources, 67; appetite theme in, 69–71; as parody of the epic, 71–75; legal and religious satire in, 75–79; Thawed Words episode in, 79–80; prologue to, 94–99; theme of health in prologue,

94–95; use of story within a story in prologue, 96; repetition in prologue, 96–97; antithesis in prologue, 98; 103, 121, 124, 129

Gargantua, 29, 31, 32–48; themes of, 32; use of riddles in, 32–33; Renaissance Humanism in, 34, 35, 36; fusion of popular and erudite in, 34; derivation of name, 34–35; use of proverbs in, 35; fruition of satire in, 36; as fusion of parody, satire, and gigantism, 38; as anticipation of Gulliver, 38; creation of the grotesque in, 41; medieval knowledge in, 42; views on war and tyrants in, 43–44; juggling of time in, 44; description of Thélème in, 45–48; 49, 52, 59, 60, 62, 66; prologue to, 86–89; use of antithesis in prologue, 86; parallelisms in prologue, 87; development of metaphors in prologue, 87–88; irony in prologue, 88; wilfull ambiguity of prologue, 88; 90, 101, 103; views on education in, 104–108; 117, 118, 127, 129, 130

Pantagruel, 17–31; sources, 18; exaggeration in, 20; as fusion of popular and epic traditions, 21; use of similes in, 22; contrast of sublime and vulgar in, 23; as attack on scholasticism, 23–25; character of Panurge in 26–28; concept of gigantism in, 29; vulgarity of, 30; 32, 34, 40, 52, 59, 60, 66, 71, 73, 76; prologue to, 82–86; use of metaphorical tableaux in prologue, 83–84; accumulation of synonyms in prologue, 85; 93, 101, 103, 117, 118, 119, 127, 129

Third Book, The, 26, 48, 49–64; structure and movement of, 49–54; sense of ambivalence in, 52; word-play in, 52–53; use of